LESSONS LEARNED IN THE LION'S DEN

Read this book to know what it was like for this modern-day Daniel to pray in the lion's den. Read it to find out what it was like for his wife, his son, and his daughter to hope and pray and feel afraid during his captivity. If you were imprisoned in a police state, you would want a son who writes, "Father, I am proud that you are here. You are in prison because of Jesus, and I am proud of you." You would cry with joy for a daughter who writes, "I picture you like a strong and mighty lion. You are also incredibly brave. You are a wonderful dad for all of us. You read the Bible so often and you always pray for us." But there is more: there is an anointing on the lessons Daniel wants to burn into your heart. Like it or not, you are going to have to fight for your sanity in a lion's den of your own; your spouse and children will go through days of trouble. Prepare your heart. Read this book.

— Bob Blincoe, US director, Frontiers

In the years I have followed the lives and ministry of Daniel Waheli and his family, I have come to regard them as examples of Christian discipleship and cross-cultural church planting at its best. Now comes this book that profoundly humbles, challenges, and motivates me. I highly recommend this book for church planters, pastors, seminary students, cross-cultural workers, and also particularly for young people who need a practical and realistic introduction to following Jesus wholeheartedly. I plan to incorporate it in my coaching and mentoring of future pastors and church planters.

— Herschel Rosser, former church planter who coaches and mentors church planters for Vineyard USA

LESSONS LEARNED IN THE LION'S DEN

IMPRISONED FOR SHARING JESUS

DANIEL WAHELI

WILLIAM CAREY
LIBRARY

Published by William Carey Library
1605 E. Elizabeth Street
Pasadena, CA 91104 | www.missionbooks.org

Mel Hughes, editor
Hugh Pindur, graphic designer

William Carey Library is a ministry of the
U.S. Center for World Mission
Pasadena, CA | www.uscwm.org

Printed in the United States of America
18 17 16 15 14   5 4 3 2 1 BP300

Library of Congress Cataloging-in-Publication Data

Waheli, Daniel.
  Lessons learned in the lion's den : Imprisoned for Sharing Jesus.
    pages cm
  Includes bibliographical references.
  ISBN 978-0-87808-622-1 -- ISBN 0-87808-622-6 1. Church development, New. 2. Missions. 3. Evangelistic work. I. Waheli, Daniel. II. Title.
  BV652.24.W345 2015
  266--dc23
                        2014016578

CONTENTS

133235

Part 2

Appendices

FOREWORD

The gospel demands suffering. Neither the Great Commission nor the great commandment can be obeyed fully without sacrifice. If Jesus is going to be super-exalted among every tribe, tongue, and people, then His representatives must be willing to be super-abased. Only the lowly can lift up and magnify Jesus without getting in the way, or attempting to share God's glory. Suffering is however a gift not a punishment. Suffering is the wondrous present of heaven which God's people so often refuse to open, and in refusing, forfeit immeasurable joy.

Daniel and his family in their simple and precious way remind us the intention of God for suffering is His glory and our joy. Daniel lives a robust and exhilarating life. To be with him and his family is to giggle, play, rejoice, and delight in the simple beauties all around us. Those that suffer well do not show it by sobriety and heaviness—those that have been privileged to represent Jesus under duress express it through gladness, balance, grace, humor, inclusiveness, and freedom.

Along with the joy of suffering, this book also affirms the centrality of character in ministry and church planting among unreached peoples*. While Daniel is a respected and eminent missiologist, his fruitfulness is based on who he is in Jesus, not in a methodology or strategy. Daniel has learned—and models for us if we are willing to accept it—that abiding in Jesus is the subterranean foundation for all service to God. This book lays out a character based approach to church planting. Intimacy with Jesus and right relationships with His body must be our starting place in mission. Methods and strategies evolve and adapt to context, but union with Christ and unity with the global church are inviolable. In an impatient age, Daniel gently reminds us to stay the course of simply walking with Jesus, allowing His Spirit to give practical and steady direction. Daniel's twelve principles for church planting (Praise, Purification, Prayer, Proclamation, Passion and Purpose, Power, Perseverance, Persecution, Proximate believers, Presence in a community, Partners, Pitfalls) are grounded in God's character and our relationship with Him.

Reading this book will lead you towards a godly jealousy for suffering and intimacy with Jesus. As you travel with Daniel and his family through their challenges, God will stir within you a longing for the intimacy they enjoy with Him and with each other. Some intimacies are only gained by difficulty yet the eternal joy that results from suffering is unparalleled. Suffering in the end is a joy, a privilege, and a certainty for all those who radically follow Jesus and long to be like Him.

Dick Brogden
Cairo, September 2013

ACKNOWLEDGMENTS

First of all I want to praise our God and Savior Jesus Christ. Romans 15:17–18: "In Christ Jesus, then, I have reason to be proud of my work for God. For I will not venture to speak of anything except what Christ has accomplished through me."

My highest appreciation goes to my dear wife who has been walking with me faithfully for all these past years.

We, Daniel and Sara, want to express our deepest gratitude to our two children who faithfully and with great joy have walked in unity with us all their lives. We have always felt that you are a great blessing and an important part of the ministry we have done together as a family. We are so proud of you and love you so much.

We as a family are so thankful for both sets of our parents who have been a great support to us all these years with prayer and encouragement and by always warmly welcoming us into their homes.

I want to say thank you to the editor of this book and her husband who have spent countless hours praying and editing to make this book what it is. I appreciate your strong commitment to us even when our family faced the challenges of prison, questioning, and expulsion. You have always been very good and encouraging friends in the Lord.

To the hundreds of people who fasted and prayed for us, we are so thankful for your loving labor which released grace upon grace in our lives. To our on- and off-the-field crisis management teams, thank you for the countless hours you spent on your knees, on the phone, and on your computers to support us practically. To our colleagues in our host country, thank you for your steadfast prayers and love-in-action. To our team, thank you for standing with us until the end. To our leaders, your coaching and mentoring has spurred us on and given us courage to weather life's storms faithfully.

A NOTE TO THE READER

In this book, I do not use our real names nor do I mention the countries where all these stories happened. I do not want to endanger by any means the local believers or the kingdom activity that is going on at this very moment. I thank you in advance for your understanding and wish you God's blessing as you read through this book and our experiences.

Words with an asterisk are further explained in Appendix 3. Appendix 2 is a summary of what I think is the best of the methods known as "Disciple Making Movements" or "Church Planting Movements" or "Jesus Movements."

My main goal in writing this book is to encourage you to start or persevere in your race with God. I know from experience that this is the most exciting and fulfilling life a person could ever choose. I have found that the many challenges along the way produce indescribable peace, joy, and hope to make us complete and holy so that we do not lack anything. If you feel like you are missing something, God tells us how to find it in His Word:

James 1:2–4 *"Count it all joy, my brothers, when you meet trials of various kinds, for you know that the testing of your faith produces steadfastness. And let steadfastness have its full effect, that you may be perfect and complete, lacking in nothing."*

If you would like to talk more about your race with God, you can contact the author of this book at joyunderpressure.waheli@gmail.com.

So that all may glorify Him,

Daniel with Sara, Ezekiel, and Lea

PART 1

1

CALLING

I grew up in Europe, and my family attended a local evangelical church. I first heard about missions in Africa when a missionary couple shared their story at my youth group. I was moved when I saw pictures of African children and felt for the first time the Holy Spirit drawing me to missions. I was fourteen years old when this happened, and though I was walking with the Lord, my commitment to Him was not very strong.

I moved on with life and studied business and administration. When I finished my studies, my friend and I had three months before we had to start our mandatory military service. Initially, we wanted to have some fun and travel around the world. In the end, however, we decided to do some mission work in Africa also. We spent most of our time in a mission hospital doing administrative and practical tasks. While I appreciated and saw the eternal value of their work, it was clear to me that this was not something I wanted to do with my life. I learned that I wanted to be directly involved in church planting among unreached peoples. I went home with a deep love for Africa and a desire to return and share the good news with people who had never had a chance to hear the gospel.

When I returned to Europe, I had some great opportunities to pursue a professional career in my home country. I told God if He wanted me to dedicate my life to cross-cultural missions among unreached peoples, He would need to direct me clearly. I began to feel a subtle but constant discontentment with the knowledge that there are people in the world who have never heard the gospel. I read biographies and books about missionaries who went to unreached peoples. The more I learned about cross-cultural ministry, the more the excitement in my heart grew. In spite of all of this, I still was not sure if this was the way the Lord wanted me to invest my life.

In 1990, I decided to devote a week to seeking God's will for my life by attending a mission's conference. There were more than 150 mission agencies represented that all needed people, but I did not feel the call of the Lord to join one of them. I needed to hear from the Lord directly, so I took a day away from the conference to pray and fast. But I did not hear anything from the Lord about missions. I thought I knew His will and planned to go back and pursue my professional career. On the last night of the conference, the speaker said that the Lord had told him that there were people in the room that the Lord wanted to call for overseas missions and that He would make their calling clear that night. When I heard those words, it was like God Himself spoke to me. I wanted to stand up and say, "Yes, here I am. I am willing to go." I was so touched by his introductory words that I didn't hear anything else that he said that night. I responded to God with a commitment to cross-cultural missions. My heart overflowed with joy, and I praised the Lord for speaking to me. I went home, quit my job, and started preparing to go back to Africa long term.

I signed up for a YWAM (Youth with a Mission)* discipleship school in Togo (West Africa). This is a school where young people get theoretical training in a classroom for three months, and then they spend three months doing outreach in another country. In preparation for my trip, I spent three months in Northern France to improve my French. While I was there, I also learned how to fast and pray for unreached peoples in Africa. One morning I felt that I should ask the Lord where in Africa I should do the outreach portion of my training. Later that day, a woman who worked in Mali (West Africa) spoke to our group. While she was speaking I said to the Lord in my heart, "If you want me to spend part of my time in Mali, then please send her to me after her talk, and let her invite me to go to Mali." When she finished her talk, she came right over to me and asked me if I wanted to go to Mali to work there. Surprised, I said, "Yes, I would." Later that evening, the older missionary couple with whom I was staying thought I would be interested in a prayer letter that they had received from a missionary couple in Mali. It was as if God was confirming what had happened earlier that morning through this letter when I saw the phrase, "The Lord has spoken today very clearly to you, go to Mali . . ." At that moment, I told the Lord that I was ready and willing to go there.

After I finished my language training in France, I went to Togo to start my YWAM school. I was excited about the first three months during which we would receive teaching during the week and do outreach on the weekends. On our outreaches, we gave our testimonies, did dramas in churches, and even preached the word of God in churches and on the streets. This was the kind of work I felt the Holy Spirit wanted me to pursue—sharing the good news with people and church planting.

After the first three months of classroom training at the Togo discipleship school, we began the process of praying about where to do the three months of outreach. Our leader felt from the Lord that we should go to three different places, one of which was Mali. The leader prayed for each student, and he put me in the Mali group. I told the leader that I was excited to go to Mali, but that I didn't have a visa and couldn't get one where we were in Togo. He said that he had prayed about this and that I should just go and not worry about the visa.

In Togo, we had worked with animists* and saw many people come to the Lord in dramatic ways. Our three-month outreach, however, started with a few weeks in Burkina Faso. This was our first time in a Muslim* village. Since Burkina Faso is a country that extends religious freedom to its people, we shared the gospel openly with the whole village present. When I preached, I talked about Revelation 21 and 22 describing the beauty of heaven. When I asked the people who would like to live in such a place, the whole village raised their hands. With joyful expectation, I explained what Jesus did to open the door for us to enter heaven. When I asked who would like to follow Jesus, not one person raised his hand. I was shocked. Had I done something wrong? Was there sin in my life that was impeding the work of the Holy Spirit? John, my translator, encouraged me to share the message again since the people might not have understood. Their reaction was the same the second time. John asked me to share it again a third time. I agreed to do it but was very embarrassed that no one was responding. After the third altar call with no response, I felt humiliated. I gave the microphone to John and disappeared into the darkness. I asked the Lord what I had done wrong, but He did not give me an answer. After a while, I went back to the place and was surprised to find that the people were still there. John had urged them to go home, but they stayed. They said that they would like to believe in Jesus, but they were unwilling to leave their tribe or endure persecution. We then had to leave the village, and people started to go home. That evening, the Holy Spirit spoke very clearly to my heart again. He said, "I want you to go and share the good news with Muslims. I love them and I want to save them. Are you willing to follow Me and go to the places I will show you?" I told the Lord that I was willing, but I would need His help and guidance. At that point in my life, I knew very little about Islam.

After two weeks, we moved on to the border of Mali. I asked the Lord what I should say and do when we arrived at the border. When we came to the border, we didn't even have to stop the car. It was a miracle. God opened the door for me to enter Mali. I got my visa easily at the police office the next day in one of the larger towns. I spent the next several months sharing the gospel with Muslims and realized that a race with God on the mission field is very exciting. He can open doors when they seem to be closed. The Lord told me that He is the boss of this work and that my job is to follow Him wherever He guides me.

When I left Mali, I realized that I needed more training and knowledge about working among Muslims. So I spent the next three years in Europe preparing for a long-term career overseas by going to Bible school and getting a bachelor's degree in missions and church planting. During this time, the Lord tested me to see if I was really willing to follow Him wherever He would lead.

2

PREPARATION

Before I went to Togo to do my discipleship training, I had asked a woman named Ruth to pray about a possible relationship with me. We agreed to pray for the next eight months and then make a decision. When I came back from Africa, she didn't have a clear yes or no. Ruth was not sure if she wanted to spend the rest of her life in Africa. This was very hard for me because I really liked her. I did not know what to do. I wrestled with this dilemma for two weeks, and I still did not know what to do. Then God reminded me clearly of what He had told me to do with my life. I told Him that I would be willing to go back to Africa even if it meant going single. Looking back, I can see this as a time when the Lord tested my heart and my commitment to the call He put on my life. I praise God that He gave me the grace to stay faithful to His calling. I told the Lord that from that point on, I would not even consider a relationship unless the woman had a call to missions independently from me. He answered my prayers sooner than I expected.

While I was in Bible school, I was part of a leadership team that did youth ministry. I noticed a woman named Sara on the leadership team who seemed very committed to loving and following the Lord. I thought she might have some feelings for me, but I was hesitant to start a relationship without knowing that she was also called by God to Africa. After a few months, I told Sara, "You are a great young woman, and I sense the Lord's presence in you. I might be wrong, but it seems like you might have some feelings for me. If this is true, please let those feelings go because I am not really interested in you. I am sorry." Sara told me that she did have some feelings for me and that she was thankful that I was honest with her.

A few months later, the Lord called Sara to go and work with Muslims in Africa. When she resigned from her job to start a two-year training program in Southern France targeting North Africans, I realized that the Lord really had called her to work with Muslims in Africa. I felt that Sara was the woman the Lord wanted to put by my side, but I also felt hesitant to share this with her after telling her very clearly not to develop any further feelings for me. I finally mustered up the courage to ask her if she would be willing to become my wife and to spend a big part of her life with me in Africa. Sara was very surprised and asked me what had changed so quickly. I explained what I had told the Lord about not starting a relationship with anyone unless she was called independently to Africa. She was very touched. We started our relationship in August and got engaged in December. Sara left for her training in Southern France in January, and we spent the next two years exchanging letters and a few very expensive phone calls since the Internet did not exist yet. I continued to work towards a bachelor of missions degree.

During my time in Bible school, I learned about three places where we could start a pioneering work among unreached Muslims. I went to Africa for about a month to seek God's will for our first place of ministry. We arrived early in the morning after having been on a truck for many hours during the night. I was very tired, and all I wanted to do was find a place to sleep. But to my surprise, a man named Hassan asked me if I was the one who would help him share the good news in this town. He had dreamed that he should go to the market place and look for a white person who would help him share the good news. Hassan was a Muslim who had recently accepted Jesus. So together we shared the good news of Jesus with some of the people in the town. Within a few days, a handful of Muslims decided to follow Jesus. I was so excited to see Muslims turning to Jesus, but at the same time the Holy Spirit spoke to me and said, "This isn't the place I want you to go. These people can do the work without you."

So I traveled to the second place and met a man called Ahmed from the tribe we were thinking of reaching for Jesus. I gave him a small booklet produced by cross-cultural workers* who worked among the same people group in a different country. When Ahmed read the first page of the booklet, he said to me in French, "I am a Muslim; you are a Christian. I am not allowed to talk to you anymore. Take this booklet and go." When I heard these words, I felt the Holy Spirit saying, "This is the people group with whom I want you to work and share My name."

I moved on and travelled to another city where this people group lived to ask God if this might be a town where we should live. I arrived there in the evening by bush taxi* and asked for a place to stay overnight. The people were very unfriendly, which is unusual for Africans, and they told me to move on and not to stay there. I looked for a taxi so that I could move on, but there were no taxis. So finally they took me to the leader of the city to ask him what they should do with me. I waited there until the man arrived at his house. His wife asked me where I had come from and what I wanted to do there. I told her that I had come from another town and would just travel through this town and move on tomorrow. When I mentioned the town from which I had come, she said that part of her family lived there. I told her that I had been invited to a wedding there a few days ago and told her the name of the bride. Suddenly, the whole situation changed. Delighted she said, "That is my cousin. You attended the wedding of my cousin. You are welcome in our city." When her husband came home, I was treated as their special guest. Over the next few days, he showed me the whole city. Once more I was delighted to see how my God is in control of everything. As I continued in my race with God, I enjoyed more and more the exciting adventure it was to work for Him advancing His kingdom.

I went back to Europe and got married to Sara in June of 1995 after a two-and-a-half-year engagement. The Lord had confirmed our calling to the country I had visited to Sara as well. Her parents had been praying with us about our ministry in this country, and my father-in-law had a clear vision of many people getting saved in the main city and from there taking the gospel back to their villages. This was actually exactly what happened years later. After our wedding, we spent another year in preparation by learning French and English and spending a few months working for our organization's sending base*.

3

A NEW CULTURE

Originally, we thought we would spend a few years focused on learning the language and culture in a relatively open country to the south of our country of ministry. However, because of an urgent situation and challenges the country faced, we were invited to move directly to the north to work with an NGO (non-governmental organization)* to serve a large number of malnourished children. We were excited to move there and probably be the first people with a clear vision and passion to plant churches among this unreached people group. We were very thankful that we were able to learn a lot from a few other couples who lived in the same city but were targeting other peoples who spoke a different language. I was not at all experienced in working with Muslims, but I learned some theories in school and had some ideas of my own. I was most afraid that we would not find the right balance in how openly we should share the gospel. We wanted to be wise and use discretion if it was needed, but we also did not want to err on the side of not sharing the gospel enough. The director of the NGO gave me some great advice on sharing the gospel in a Muslim context. He told me to share the gospel with every Muslim I meet within the first five minutes. After all, that is the reason that we are here. He also advised against talking about politics or speaking negatively about anything related to their religion as this would create a lot of problems. This advice was very

> He told me to share the gospel with every Muslim I meet within the first five minutes. After all, that is the reason that we are here.

helpful, and I still use these principles to share Jesus wherever I am. I pray for the political leaders and situations, but I do not get involved in discussions on these topics.

We felt it was important to live among the people we were trying to reach. Our area did not have a realtor, so we just walked around and asked the local shopkeepers if they knew of a room for rent. I found a good possibility, but the husband, David, was not around, so I had to return later that evening. They had a room available in their house, but I felt that it was not the right place for us. David was a tailor, and I asked him to make me some local clothes, which he did happily. Later on, he became one of the first believers from this people group. David confessed years later that he had not wanted to rent me a room because he was afraid that I was a spy sent to his house to see what he was doing. He came from an oppressed people group that had experienced some very difficult years just before we arrived.

We finally found a room to rent that shared the compound with about forty other people in eight different rooms. We all shared the same shower and the same bathroom. In the summer time, we all slept outside because the tin roof made it too hot inside. The house did not have electricity or running water, so we got our water from a donkey cart that came daily to our compound and delivered the water to each family. While sleeping outside with forty other people did not provide much privacy, the Lord used this circumstance to help us better understand the people and their daily challenges.

Thankfully, the rainy season was short because water often entered our compound and sometimes our room. Sara and I experienced challenges that we had never before encountered. I was very proud of her as she handled this simple life so well. We had one small gas bottle in our room for cooking, two simple mattresses for sleeping, a bucket for the drinking water, and an iron wardrobe for our clothes.

We chose this lifestyle because most of the people we wanted to reach lived this way. It gave us great access to the people, and the Lord helped us learn the language and culture quickly. Our great difficulty in not having a lot of privacy was also our chance to be a bright light for Jesus. It was impossible to hide anything from the neighbors. The walls were too thin. We all knew each other's lives well. Sometimes when there was a fight between neighbors or husband and wife, I had to take the man away and ask him to forgive the other person so that he would stop beating his wife or the neighbor. The tradition was that one could not stop fighting until a third party separated the fighters. Once, one of our neighbors said, "You never ever beat your wife. What do you do that your wife is still so humble and respects you as her husband? We need to beat our wives regularly to keep them obedient to us." Another man said, "Your wife is a godly wife. She must love God so much. The way she lives and treats you and the rest of us shows me that she fears God very much."

We were very thankful that we were able to live in this place that provided many opportunities to meet people easily, to learn the language and the culture, and to be a testimony for Jesus. We believe that our fruitfulness for the kingdom in that country and our next country of service were in large part due to this season. The language skills and cultural understanding we gained have been so valuable over our years of ministry.

> Our commitment to live with people is not the key to winning people's hearts. The Holy Spirit has to touch people so that they can understand who Jesus is.

However, the greatest gain during this time was that we learned to love the people in a way that we wouldn't have if we had not lived as one of them. It is interesting, however, that no one except for one woman from this compound accepted the Lord Jesus. We realized that our commitment to live with those people is a great way to be close with the local community, but it is not the key to winning people's hearts. The Holy Spirit has to touch people so that they can understand who Jesus is.

4

FRUIT

During our eighteen months living on the compound, our team usually fasted one day a week and prayed once a week for five hours for God's power to come down. We also prayed daily as a team for an hour to see God's mighty hand touch these wonderful people. After three months, God gave us the first believers. Most of them just came to us through God's supernatural guidance.

One day, a poor lady named Lydia selling bananas on the side of the road stopped us and said, "Are you the ones who have come to give me a book that I should read to find the truth?" We were astonished and asked her why she asked us such a question. She then told us that when she was ten years old, she had had a dream in which she saw my wife and one of our teammates giving her a book. We had the Gospel of Luke with us, so we gave it to her. Lydia read it very fast and was ready to follow Jesus after a very short time. Later, she told us that when she had had this dream as a child, her father took her to a local, respected religious leader because she was very disturbed by this dream. When this man heard her dream, he said to the father, "Your daughter is cursed to follow Jesus one day, and there is nothing you or I can do. Just wait and see. Lydia will follow Jesus one day. Take your daughter and go home." Fifteen years later, the daughter became one of the first women in this tribe to follow Jesus.

Another evening, a man named Hussein came after sunset to our compound and seemed afraid. He took a copy of the Gospel of Luke out of his pocket and said, "I want to follow this, but I am afraid of the people and the whole society around me. Please help me to understand more about Jesus and teach me how to follow Him here in this society." Hussein reminded me of Nicodemus in the third chapter of John. He later brought some of his friends to me and some of them accepted the Lord as well. Most of these young men, though, did not stay with us. They wanted to travel abroad to look for a better life than what their country had to offer. That was hard for us to accept since it felt like a big hit on our church planting efforts. The first believers were leaving the country. But we learned to trust the Lord and to be obedient in sharing the good news with those the Lord brought to us.

Later we met a man named Omar from a higher class who had spent several years traveling abroad. We met him after he had settled down and had several children. He was a very humble man, and I felt from the beginning that he was a man of peace. We spent a lot of time together, and I also got to know his eldest son, Yaquub. Both of them started reading the New Testament, and one day Yaquub asked me what he had to do to follow Jesus. We agreed that he would have to ask his father first, and I offered to talk with him about it as well. When I talked with Omar, he said, "I would be proud if Yaquub were to follow the teachings of Jesus as this book says, because then he would be a godly man." A few months later both of them accepted Jesus, and they were among the first men to be baptized.

During this season we fully realized that it is indeed the Holy Spirit who prepares the hearts of people. He needs to open the eyes of men and women to help them understand who Jesus is. What a great joy it was to see the first men and women be baptized in the name of Jesus.

5

THE UNSEEN WORLD

We were strong in our conviction that the Lord is always in control, but we were growing in our understanding that the devil is not going to easily let people go without trying to keep them in darkness. The people group with whom we were working was 100 percent Muslim, but almost all of them were involved in a form of occultism called Folk Islam*.

On one occasion, Hawa, one of our neighbors, had a fight with her husband Mustafa and ran away. Mustafa told Hawa if she didn't come back by the end of the month, something bad would happen to her. Hawa didn't go back, and Mustafa went to the local witch doctor to curse her with insanity. On the last day of the month in the middle of the night, Hawa lost her mind.

Another time, a man brought us his demonized son who was in chains. With prayer and some medical treatment, he got much better. In spite of our encouragement to follow Jesus and receive full deliverance from the demons, the family did not want to surrender their lives to Jesus. So we actually stopped praying for him, for, as the Bible says, if a house is cleansed but not filled with something else, seven more terrible spirits will enter. A few weeks later, the man's son ended up in the same condition—demonized and in chains in their house.

After a few weeks of reading the Bible with a man well versed in the Koran named Abdallah, we read about Jesus setting people free from demons. Abdallah told me that he wanted to show me his life insurance. I was surprised to hear of an African with life insurance, but it wasn't long before I understood what he meant. He brought me a shirt full of charms and Koranic verses. Abdallah had inherited this from his father, and its value was a year's salary. He said that he wanted to burn this shirt because he now trusted in the Lord. We went to the beach to burn the shirt. We took with us from the same tribe a few younger men who had recently started following the Lord. The younger men said that the shirt was too powerful to be burned and that it would jump out of the fire. It was used in the early days of war to protect people from guns and knives. We prayed in the name of Jesus and set it on fire. All these young believers saw that Jesus is more powerful than the power that they used to follow. We found out later that fifteen miles away, Abdallah's wife, not knowing what was happening on the beach, felt her spirit power leave her house. When she searched for the shirt in the house and didn't find it, she knew it was burning.

Another person came to us frustrated that he was not able to move ahead in his new faith. He started to confess horrible sexual sins in his life through which he had opened the door for the demons to enter. When he confessed his sins, the Lord delivered him completely and gave him victory over the darkness. Today he is married and has a family.

Zeinab, a woman who had come from another Arab country but was married locally, became good friends with my wife Sara. Together they watched a version of the Jesus Film* about Mary from Magdalene* specially made for women. The film clearly depicts how Mary was possessed by demons and then how Jesus set her free. After the film, Zeinab confessed that she was demon possessed. She even remembered how the evil spirits entered her life when she was twelve years old. By that time, we had more experience in dealing with evil spirits, and we knew that we should only pray for her to be delivered if she was willing to accept Jesus and surrender her whole life to Him. Zeinab did not want to do this, so we prayed for her,

> If they only experience the power of Jesus without getting to know the truth of Jesus, they will not follow Him.

but didn't cast out the demon. After the prayer, she confessed that she realized another power was at work when we prayed. We told her that she could be fully delivered but that she would have to surrender her life to Jesus. Zeinab was not willing to do so and is still under the demonic influence.

Another time we shared the gospel in a village area, and the people seemed to be very open. We prayed for the sick, and the Lord started to move and touch people. Suddenly, a woman started to make noise like a tiger and approached my friend and me saying, "This is the last time you are going to speak and proclaim the name of Jesus. I am here to kill you now." We said that Satan is a liar, and Jesus conquered him on the cross. We prayed in the name of Jesus, and suddenly, the woman fell down like a dead person. She lay there for about five minutes and then stood up totally healed. The people were more open to hear the gospel after they had seen that God's power is greater than the evil occult forces they all knew and feared.

We prayed for barren women as well. Some of them were cursed, and others just didn't conceive for reasons we did not know. In several cases, God gave the women children.

Many other stories could be added to the ones above. I just wanted to mention a few to emphasize the importance of knowing the power of Jesus in our lives as we enter into the battle with the unseen world. Praise the Lord that we are victorious as Jesus is the ultimate victor! Power encounters are often a door opener for people to hear about Jesus. But it is crucial that people have a truth encounter with Jesus as well. If they only experience the power of Jesus without getting to know the truth of Jesus, they will not follow Him.

6

THREATS AND CHALLENGES

The people with whom we worked were some of the friendliest people I have ever met. They were very welcoming and quickly invited foreigners into their homes to share meals and everything they had. Even though they were strictly Muslim, they were open to people from different religions, especially Christians. This had not always been the case. Hundreds of years ago, these were the people who brought Islam to many tribes in West Africa. They were considered the pure and holy followers of Islam. In recent history, their religious pride was broken by ethnic cleansing that started in 1989. Muslims who were lighter in color killed and persecuted other Muslims because of their ethnic background. Many of these formerly proud African Muslims* started to be open to new ideas. They met people from the West who helped them. One of my friends, who was a religious leader, told me, "If you had come here ten years ago, I would not have even greeted you because you are not a Muslim. But I have seen how you have helped my tribe, even if you are a Christian."

Even though we made many friends, some of the people from this tribe and other tribes were not happy with our presence there. Over a span of ten years, our team received several intimidating and threatening letters, some of which we took seriously. A common practice in this country was that the messenger bringing us these threats would ask for money in exchange for more information. We did not take these kinds of threats seriously and assumed that the messenger was just trying to get money from us.

One of the threats that we took seriously came to a friend of mine and me just a few days after Sara and my son Ezekiel had returned to our home country because of medical issues in Sara's pregnancy. A man came to our office and barged into a meeting, refusing to leave until he had spoken with me. He told me that he overheard sixteen men plan to "slaughter us like lambs." We knew this threat was serious because he did not want any money. Since the American embassy had saved his life fifteen years earlier, he had vowed to help all of the white foreigners that he could.

We felt scared. Our first reaction was to get on the first plane out of there, but we realized that this path would mean that we would be leaving our host country for good. Leaving for a few weeks and coming back would not change the situation at all. After praying and talking with Sara on the phone, we decided to stay. That night, my friend and I lay on the roof and reflected on how we had lived our thirty-three years so far. The one thing that we both felt clearly was that we would again lay down our lives for Jesus and vow to serve Him wherever He wanted us to go. There is no greater joy than to be in the will of our Lord Jesus. The Lord spoke to us through Psalm 91:7 which became one of my life verses.

Psalm 91:7
"A thousand may fall at your side, ten thousand at your right hand, but it will not come near you."

The Lord spoke deep into our hearts and made this truth alive. Amazing peace filled our hearts. We knew deeply in our hearts that nothing could happen to us at the hands of men unless the Lord allowed it. This meant that the Lord would also be responsible for the consequences, namely taking care of my family.

I am not saying that people should never flee the risk of persecution. We see in Paul's life that sometimes he escaped his persecutors by fleeing, and in other situations he decided to stay even if it meant persecution and death. He was led by the Holy Spirit to know what he should do in each of the situations he faced. In the same way, we felt that since the Lord had spoken to us on that roof, we knew that the Lord would be in charge of our families and us no matter what the results were.

We took this information about the possible attack on us to the local police. They were very concerned because they did not want any foreigners to get hurt as this would have a negative impact on their international relationships. They investigated the matter, but found none of the sixteen men. So we continued on with life, and nothing ever happened to our bodies. In our spirits, however, that which Satan meant for evil actually strengthened our faith in the One who is sovereign over everything.

A couple of years later, my faith in God to protect my family was tested again when my name and the names of key Muslim background believer (MBB)* leaders appeared in the local newspaper in a story about our church planting work. The article said that I was the most dangerous person in the country because I had converted over 150 people to Christianity. The article also linked me to another situation in which an African pastor had allegedly kidnapped a young MBB woman. We found out about this article while we were in our home country on furlough* a week before we were planning to return to our host country. Again, we found ourselves praying about whether or not to risk my life by returning. The Lord spoke to us as a family, and we felt that the Lord wanted us to return and to stand with the local believers. Our church leaders agreed with our decision, so we went.

I really had to fight against worry over my family if I were to be killed or imprisoned for many years and about the MBBs and their families. Our stress was compounded when this newspaper continued to print articles about us almost weekly. But we continued to walk in faith in the One who promised me that "a thousand may fall at your side, ten thousand at your right hand, but it will not come near you."

Most of what the newspaper printed about us was true, but one week they printed an article that was unquestionably erroneous. The article accused us of homosexual activity, which was severely punished in this culture. We took this article to a well-connected friend of ours who was shocked to read such lies. A few days later, this same newspaper mysteriously shut down for two years.

Another challenging "security" situation that we experienced in this country came as a result of being exposed by Osman, an MBB who was working with us on a very important evangelistic translation project. He was the voice for the film that we believed would be a tool for God to save many more people from this people group. We had just finished recording and were ready to move on to the production of this movie when Osman was stopped by the border police on his way to the neighboring country to visit his family. The police questioned him after finding a Bible in his bag and threatened him with prison and death. After a few days, they told him that they knew about all the people with whom he worked and promised him freedom if he would tell them the names of the people. Believing their lies, Osman told them the whole story of how he came to follow Jesus and about his vision to see hundreds of people come to know Jesus through the film that we had translated into the local language. He mentioned that he got to know Jesus because of me and that I was the head of an organization. When he finished sharing, the police commissioner was very angry and said, "I have recorded all of your confessions on this tape here. You will be judged and go to prison and this organization will be kicked out of the country." Osman had fallen into the commissioner's trap and revealed everything. They took his passport and sent him back to his home.

He immediately came to see me and told me the whole story. While I was disappointed that he had been so easily trapped by the police, I told him how proud I was that he had not denied his faith. I also told him that we had been through other challenging situations such as this one and that he should not be afraid because God was with us. We prayed together that the Lord would intervene and help us overcome this challenge through His power. Osman left the office confident that the Lord would help us.

A few days later the police called him to see if they could get some money out of him by telling him that they would keep the whole thing secret if he would give them a large sum of money. He knew by now that the police were just lying and that they would never close the file. He told them that they would not get any money and that the Lord we trusted was with us, so we would not be afraid of them. The police officer got very upset and said, "I will show you that your God will not be able to help you. This organization will be kicked out." Osman came back to me and said that the commissioner wanted to act quickly and that he was determined to act on what he had decided. He asked me for some money so that one of his uncles who had influence could help us. We looked together at the Bible, and I explained to him why we couldn't do this, even if it was acceptable and normal in his culture. The whole situation became a discipleship lesson for him.

This time Osman left frightened. I saw fear take over, and he was still upset that I would not give him money for his uncle to resolve the problem for us. The same night he called me and said that he would commit suicide if we could not give his uncle the money. I told him that I could not give his uncle money and that he should not destroy his life and his eternity by killing himself. I did not sleep much that night and prayed that God would help him overcome the attack from the evil one. Thanks be to God that he didn't commit suicide. As it came closer to the time that they wanted to take us to court and judge our work and put him in prison, Osman's father asked his uncle to do something because it would bring much shame on their family and even on the whole tribe if his son were to be openly judged for having become a follower of Jesus. God used the father's fear of shame to resolve the threat for us. The police commissioner closed the file to avoid shaming the whole tribe.

Although life-threatening security situations were very challenging for both of us, for my wife they proved to be the single most difficult part about taking the gospel to another culture. In each circumstance, however, God used these situations to make us more dependent on Him and to prepare us little by little for the works He had appointed for our family.

Our team grew, the development work continued well, and the church planting work spread to other towns and villages in the country. At a conference I was attending, the Lord spoke to me about the needs in one of the largest nations in Africa that still had more than one hundred unreached Muslim people groups. I felt the Holy Spirit clearly speak to my heart that we should move on to this country as our next place of ministry. I shared this with my wife, and we started to pray about it. The Lord spoke to us that we should only leave when three things were in place: a good team leader, someone with a vision to take over the development work, and a commission to the next country from the local MBB church. The first two criteria were met quickly. A very gifted leader was willing to lead the team and take over the development work as well. The third point was more of a challenge. I shared the idea with the local elders of the MBB church, and they all felt that it would be too early for me to go and that I should stay a bit longer. So we agreed and stayed for another two years, during which I was able to turn over most of my local responsibilities and start to train church planters internationally.

One evening, the security police arrested Sheikh, one of the local elders in the MBB church. They first came to his house in uniform. When his wife told them that he was suffering from malaria, they left. An hour later, they returned in plain clothes and arrested him even though he was very sick and weak. When he was released, Sheikh called me right away wanting to see me in a private place. He told me that security knew everything. They knew that I led him and others to the Lord, and they seemed like they were going to take action. He told me he was convinced that the time for my family and me in this country had come to an end and that we should go to the next place of ministry. Sheikh said that if we went now, we could always come back on short trips, but if we were kicked out, we might not be able to return. It seemed like the Lord used this security situation to fulfill the third criterion of being commissioned to the next place by the local church.

It was not easy for us to leave the place and the people we loved so much. Years ago, we left our home country with a firm commitment to stay in that country our whole lives if it were necessary for the church to be planted there. We praise God for his work among this people. In spite of the many difficulties that the newly established church faced in the years after we left, the work of church planting continues. God reminded us that, ultimately, the work is His and that He does it through different people over many different seasons.

7

A NEW COUNTRY

We arrived at the new place and felt overwhelmed by the enormous need to see all these precious, unreached Muslim peoples reached with the gospel. In our previous country, we were focused on one people group. In our new country, we found ourselves faced with the challenge of more than a hundred tribes that needed Jesus. However, we also found a strong church imbedded in the culture that could be mobilized to reach out and share the good news with Muslims if the Christians would be able to overcome and forgive the decades of pain, persecution, and suffering received from the very people who needed the love of Jesus the most. In time, the Holy Spirit worked in the hearts of some key leaders in the church and birthed a desire in them to reach out to Muslims.

Two years before I arrived, a man who was very influential in his denomination wrote a proposal to his denomination with his vision to reach out to Muslims. It was rejected by the other leaders. When I arrived in the country and shared my heart with him, he told me about his vision from the Lord, and he told me he wanted to do something with that vision. He organized a month-long training on sharing Jesus with Muslims, contextualizing the gospel message for them and planting house churches. The Lord touched the hearts of many during the training, and the first twenty church planters were sent to unreached tribes with the blessing of all the leadership. We did more training, and over eighty people were sent out or simply returned to their own cities after having traveled to the training. We had just seen the first house church come from these trainings when a war broke out, and many people, including some of the church planters themselves, had to flee to refugee camps. It looked like the enemy had destroyed a lot of what had been started, but the war actually opened hearts among some unreached Muslim tribes that previously had been closed to the gospel. These Muslim tribes were attacked by the Arab Muslim* government because of their ethnic background, and as a result, they became disillusioned with Islam. One tribe of fifteen thousand people came as a whole to Christian leaders and told them that they would like to know more about Jesus. Clearly these people didn't understand what it meant to follow Jesus, but their openness to at least hear the gospel was greater than ever before. We will only know in heaven how many people entered the kingdom because of the persecution they received. I greatly rejoiced to see local Christians reaching out to their close Muslim neighbors with the good news.

While we were training local Christians to reach out to Muslims, some like-minded colleagues and I started an educational business to enable other expatriate workers* like myself to serve the people by teaching them English. Our goal was to start ten branches of the business in the least reached cities of our country. After a couple of years, we finally got all the paperwork completed and opened our first three centers. It was amazing to see hundreds of students come daily to learn English. After the English classes, we had a place where people could sit and drink tea and practice their English. The conversation often turned to spiritual topics and the Lord used these opportunities to share the good news with many people. In one of the centers, quite a few people came into the kingdom. In the other two centers, we sowed seeds and expected to see visible fruit in the future.

As a side note, I have traveled a lot around the world, and it seems that educational centers* are a great door opener to contact many people, to bless them as we teach them English, and to talk with them about Jesus. I would recommend this business to many people all over the world. It seems that many people from unreached tribes are eager to learn English because this opens up the opportunity for them to get a job with international organizations and creates other opportunities throughout the English speaking world.

We had another five team leaders ready to start more educational centers in our country when the government changed its policy toward Christian workers. Many like-minded businesses were shut down, including ours, and over two hundred people had to leave the country in late 2012 and early 2013.

8

THE FIRST DETAINMENT

The story of my imprisonment and expulsion actually starts in late 2010 so I must back up a little bit and explain some of the events leading up to it. Part of my work is overseeing team leaders within our organization. This requires that I make several international "coaching" trips every year to meet with them and come alongside the church planting work they are doing. In late 2010, I took my son Ezekiel with me on a coaching trip. I wanted to show him what I did on these trips. We really had a great time together and my son was a blessing to the children in the families we visited. It also showed Ezekiel another aspect of missionary life, which was beneficial since his dream right now is to take the gospel by horse or camel to one of the least reached tribes in the world. It was a very special trip for both of us.

We arrived at three a.m. exhausted from the long journey. We were bumped off of our original flight because a West African president bought out the whole plane for himself, and all the passengers were taken to a hotel until the new flight the next day. Although it was fun to have a surprise vacation day, we arrived a day later than we had planned. By the time we got our luggage, we were very ready to be home, but we were stopped by a man running after us yelling, "Are you Daniel?" He asked us to follow him, and we were taken to a security office. When we arrived there they started to ask us strange questions like, "Where are you from? Where have you come from? When did you last leave the country? How many years have you lived in this country? Why are you here? What are your activities here?" etc. I knew they already had all the answers to their questions. Over an hour later, they released us but kept our passports and asked me to come back the next day. I politely asked them if I could come in three days because it was the twenty-third of December, and I didn't want to spend Christmas in the security offices. They accepted this and asked me to return on the twenty-sixth of December. Thinking that the questioning was routine, we left and were not worried at all.

On the morning of the twenty-sixth during my usual time with the Lord, I heard a voice in my heart say "Daniel, today they will ask you to the leave the country with your family, but you should not accept their words. You should stay." When I had this thought in my heart, I was not sure if it was the Holy Spirit or just my own imagination, but it was strong enough that I took it seriously in prayer. I felt that I should not leave the country unless they gave me a legitimate reason to do so. I decided to take Ezekiel with me since he also had been present when we had arrived at the airport, and they had confiscated both of our passports.

When we arrived at the airport, we were taken to a special office where I met the "big man" who again asked me the same questions that I had been asked a few days prior. We answered him the same way we answered the last time. We tried to be polite, but I also let my tone of voice convey that I was not happy with the way they were treating us. At the end, he told me that my family and I had seven days to leave the country and that we should not return. Now I knew for sure that the Holy Spirit had spoken to me that morning, and I was prepared for this exact situation. I asked the man politely what I had done wrong to be asked to leave like this. He said that he did not know the reason. He was just delivering the message from the "big" people. I asked him, "May I speak with these big people? I would like to know why I have to leave your country that my family and I love so much. I have started two businesses with other partners and cannot just leave the country within seven days without any clear reason." He then told me that it was impossible to see these people and that I should go home and leave the country within seven days. I kindly replied that I would go home now but that I would not leave the country until they gave me legitimate reason to leave. I also told him that many people from his country lived in my home country and that they would never be asked to leave in this manner. He was unimpressed by my arguments and repeated his request. I told them again that I would not leave without a valid reason. We repeated the same conversation once more, but this time I added that they would have to come and take me to the airport by force. This is the way we parted, and I went home with our passports.

When I arrived at home and told Sara what had happened, I realized what I had done. I began to second-guess myself and the way I had interacted with these men. Was my response from the Spirit or my flesh? I consulted with two friends whom I respect very much—a local pastor and a cross-cultural worker* who had been in the country for more than fifteen years and who had undergone similar threats and challenges. Both friends felt that my reaction came from the Lord and that I should not leave the country. I received this as an affirmation of my response, and we decided to stay. Sara packed our things, and the children decided which of their things they wanted to take with us just in case they forced us to leave.

Nothing happened until the seventh day when, suddenly, early in the morning a police car stopped right in front of our door. We waited for him to come in, but nobody came. After an hour, I could not wait any longer and decided to go out to ask him what he wanted from us. I asked him what I could do for him. He said, "Oh sir, I am so sorry. I hope that my car didn't disturb you. I just visited my older sister, and this was the only parking spot I could find. I hope it did not bother you." Fully relieved and thankful to God I said, "No problem at all. You can keep your car here as long as you would like. It does not disturb me at all." We praised the Lord that nothing happened after this, and we continued to live and work as before.

9

THE SECOND ARREST

I continued to share the gospel as much as possible, and about three months later, I met Abdul while I was waiting for my ticket outside of a travel agency. We drank tea together and continued our talk. He seemed open to the gospel, and we agreed to meet later to continue our discussion. We started reading the Bible together, and he told me that he wanted to believe in Jesus. We met a few times more, and then he called me on the phone to ask for some more Bibles for his friends. Although I was not very pleased that he asked this question on the phone, I agreed to meet him.

Five minutes after Abdul arrived at my house, security also came and arrested both of us. Six men came in a pick-up truck, and four of them carried guns. They entered our house and made both of us sit down on the floor, so I could not let anyone else know that they were taking me. Sara and the kids were in the kitchen doing homework. Praise be to God that I didn't usually wear shoes inside the house, so they allowed me to go get my shoes. This gave me a chance to inform my wife in our mother tongue that I was being arrested. She thought I was joking, and I told her to come and see. Abdul and I were both taken to the security office and then immediately separated from each other. I never found out whether Abdul was seriously seeking the Lord or if he was an undercover security worker.

I was taken to the same man that had questioned me at the airport a few months earlier. He started asking me the same questions all over again as before. I asked him if I could call my wife to inform her that I was fine and tell her where I was. I wanted to make sure she knew I was taken by security and not a fundamentalist group. Initially, he refused to let me call Sara. I probably asked about twenty times before he finally acquiesced and let me call her and tell her that we would be stopping by our apartment in half an hour. I knew that there would be several people at our apartment because we had originally invited some friends to dinner. I told Sara that they should all leave.

Later, I learned that one of my closest friends, Jack, and his wife Janice, come to the apartment to support Sara when they heard what had happened. All of our dinner guests left immediately as Sara asked, but Jack and Janice felt the Lord had told them to stay and to help my wife and kids. The Lord had already called them to minister in another country in the future, so they felt that their presence in our apartment would not endanger them even if they had to leave a bit earlier than planned. They were not even from the same organization as we were. We had developed a deep friendship over the past five years and worked together sharing the same vision to see Jesus glorified throughout the country. I was very proud of them.

We arrived at our apartment, and they began their search. During this time, my friend and his wife played with our kids, which was such a blessing. Although they realized what was happening, they seemed to be quiet and have the peace of God. The security officers took twenty Bibles in Arabic and ten in English and some in our mother tongue. They took other books including our kids' picture Bibles. They also wanted to take Sara's and my laptops so that they could search them as well. They put them on the table with all the books. Even though our computers required passwords, I knew that they could force me to give them the password, and I didn't want them to see the information on our computers. I quickly told Sara that we should exchange our laptops with the kids' laptops. I asked the men if I could put our computers in a bag so that they wouldn't be destroyed by the dust and dirt, and this gave my friend Jack time to successfully switch the laptops. When they finished their search, they took me back to the security office. I was questioned some more, and then they took me home around 1 a.m. They told me that they would be back at 8 a.m. the next morning to take me back to the security office. It was the grace of God that I could go home that night.

They took me to the office the next morning as promised and began the same line of questioning again. This time, the man questioning me was clearly demonized. He was very angry with me and yelled that I was a liar and that I should tell them the truth. I started to speak in tongues and prayed against the evil spirits in this man while he continued to accuse me of being a liar. After about five minutes, the power of evil was broken. His eyes changed, and he started to behave like a man. He continued to ask me questions, but I felt that the evil power had been broken because he was behaving normally and accepted my answers. When they questioned my frequent travel, I told them that I was a businessman, and as an international consultant, I had to travel a lot. I also told them that I loved Jesus and that He was the most important person in my life because He had forgiven my sins and had given me new life. One of the lower level security men asked me if I was a "machinery." I really didn't understand and asked him what he meant. He then said that he thought that I was a man who talked to people about God which would make me a "machinery." I realized that he meant to say "missionary." I told him that every true believer, whether Muslim or Christian, should be able to testify about his faith. If this was what he meant, then yes, I was a missionary.

I had to go back to the security office every day for seven days. They mostly had me sit in a room by myself. They looked at the computers, searched the books and probably interviewed our neighbors. After this seven-day period, the main security man told me that I could go home for good today, but first he needed to take me to another office to register my passport. When I arrived, I soon realized that they were now officially arresting me. They took my watch, bag, phone, and belt, and put me in a room without allowing me to inform anybody. I was afraid that they would put me in prison without giving me the chance to tell my wife where I was. After a few minutes, the head commissioner took me into his office and started to interrogate me. He asked me the same kinds of questions, but he focused more on my faith and my religious activities. I told him that I was a businessman who loved Jesus and that I would share the truth of Jesus with anybody who would like to know. He told me that this was an Islamic country, not Europe. I shared that Jesus lived in my heart and that I would talk to anybody about Him who would like to know, whether I was in Africa or in Europe. I told him that many locals talk to me about Islam and Mohamed and the Koran. Why should I not be allowed to talk to them about Jesus? Even the Koran* confirms that it is good for every Muslim to know the words of Jesus and to read the Injil (New Testament). During our dialogue, I was able to share the good news with him. He wrote it all down on a piece of paper and then asked me to sign it. I asked him to read what he wrote before I would sign the paper. He started to read in a loud voice what it meant to become a believer. He also wrote down that I was distributing Bibles in the market place, which was not true. I told him that I would give anybody a Bible who wanted one, but I didn't say that I was distributing Bibles in the market. So the commissioner tore up the paper and rewrote the whole testimony without the part about Bible distribution. I signed the paper and was taken back to the room. I didn't know what would happen next.

Later, they asked me if I had two local friends who could be guarantors for me. I asked Jack, who had helped Sara and the kids when security had come to our flat, to help me find these two people. Two of his close friends, who really loved the Lord, humbly said that it would be a joy for them to be my guarantors as we are all a family in Christ. I was very proud of the way they loved Jesus by standing with me even though I was from a different continent. When they signed for me as guarantors, I was released the same day, but they kept the passports of my whole family. After a few weeks and several more security visits, we got the passports back for my wife and the kids, but they kept my passport so that I would not be able to leave the country. This went on for weeks. We found a lawyer, and I went back to the police station to ask for my passport so that I could return to my home country for a short time to celebrate my father's seventy-fifth birthday. With a lot of prayer and several more meetings, they agreed to let me go home for my father's birthday, but if I didn't return within one month, the two guarantors would be arrested. I confirmed that I would be back as my business was there, my kids were in school, and we loved the country.

It was not easy to understand their thinking. First they wanted me out of the country, and now they wanted to make sure that I would come back. Well, we did come back and lived uneventfully for more than a year. The lawyer said that they would have a year to take me to court, but after a year the whole case would be considered finished. They said that they would take me to court and judge me, but they never did. We rejoiced at the one-year mark when nothing had happened. Our visas were renewed, and we continued to work normally. We enjoyed the growth of our business, and more and more people were interested in joining the work. We also saw more people enter the kingdom.

10

PRISON

Eighteen months after my first encounter with security, the police came to our English center* to ask some questions. This was not alarming since the local security came for visits every once in awhile to check our work, but it was a bit strange that they came in plain clothes after 5 p.m. when our office was closed. They told me that it would only take thirty minutes and that I would be back for dinner. They then took me to an office where I was asked strange questions about my being in the country and my other activities. At this point, I realized that this was not just a routine security visit. That evening, the main security officer came to the office and wanted to read the report. A power cut prevented him from reading the report, so I had to spend the night there. The next morning the man read the report and asked me more questions. While I was waiting for a few more hours and expecting to be released, they were getting permission from the courts to search our office. About twenty security officials and I traveled back to the office, and they started their search. Two of our local workers and one of our expatriate staff members were there when we arrived. They searched everything, including the computers, but didn't find anything of interest.

Not satisfied with the results of this search, they asked me to open the door of the apartment next to the office as well. Because it was a branch manager's private flat that he and his family used whenever they came to the capital, I didn't have the key. I told them that their cleaning lady had a key that we could obtain in less than half an hour. They didn't believe me and got very angry and started to break down the door. It took them close to thirty minutes to open the door because it was a door with several security locks. When they finally succeeded, they started to search the apartment. They found about 130 MP3 players that were loaded with the word of God in five minority languages of unreached tribes in the country. Now they seemed to be satisfied with their search. While they were packing up all the MP3 players, I was able to use the cell phone of one of the workers in the office, and I called my wife from the bathroom to warn her that we would probably be coming to the educational center and to our apartment. This gave her an hour or so to prepare our apartment to be searched.

We left the building with the office and the branch manager's apartment and went to the building with the educational center and my apartment. They searched the center and briefly searched our flat, but they didn't seem to find anything. They were satisfied with the MP3 players.

I asked the officer to let me go to my house to brush my teeth because I hadn't been able to do this for more than twenty-four hours. After I had asked several times, he agreed to go with me to our apartment where I had a few minutes with my wife. I brushed my teeth, and my wife prepared a bag with my Bible, toothpaste, and a toothbrush. I gave her a short summary of what had happened. We both knew that this could be serious. When they asked me for my computer, I gave them my son's computer as I had done previously. Then we left my home. I didn't know it then, but that would be my last time there.

They took me to a different part of the security department. It was a big building, and as we entered, I realized that I was being officially arrested. They asked me a few questions and then took my ring, my watch, my belt, and everything but my toothbrush and toothpaste. I tried to keep my Bible, but the officer got very angry and took it away. When they tried to take my glasses away, I acted like I couldn't see anything at all without glasses, and they gave them back to me. I was taken in a car with black windows to the next place—the official prison. From that point on, I was treated like a real prisoner. They did a blood test and took me to a cell with a thin mattress on which to sleep.

Since I hadn't slept much in the last two days, I fell asleep quickly. I was in shock and did not really understand what had happened. The next day the soldier came to see me in the morning and asked me if I needed anything. I answered him, "Yes, for sure. I have three requests. I want to know why I am here. I want my Bible back, and I want to talk with my wife." The man said,

"Do you need anything else?" I felt quite encouraged at that time even though I doubted that they would meet my requests.

When the guard left, I started to ask God to give me the strength needed to be a witness for Him and to take care of my wife and the children. It was hard, but at this point, I was still hoping that this would all be over in a few days. When I started to look around in the cell, I saw writing on the walls. One of the writings said, "Oh, God, this is my third cell, and it has been more than five months. Please, help me to get out of here." These words hit me like a ton of bricks, and I realized that this might last for more than just a few days.

I started to pray and asked the Lord what I should be doing. I really felt the Lord tell me that I should fast. When they brought me breakfast, I refused it and said that God had told me to fast. They seemed to accept this since daytime fasting is a very important practice in their religion. I continued to pray, and the Lord was indeed close to me. After sunset, they again brought me food, which I refused because I was fasting. The guard came back with one of the higher prison officers, and they asked me why I was fasting. I told them that I was fasting because God had told me to fast. They asked me how long I would fast, and I told them, "For as long as God tells me to." After quite a long talk about faith, I convinced them that I was not on a hunger strike, and they left me alone. The next morning, a soldier came and asked me what I needed. Knowing that my requests would probably be denied again, I gave him the same answer. A few hours later the doctor came and checked my blood pressure. I promised them again that I was not on a hunger strike and that I was just praying and fasting to seek God's presence.

That afternoon, they opened my cell door and asked me to come with them. I was blindfolded and handcuffed and accompanied by several soldiers to a car. They took me to another security office where I was asked the same kinds of questions. They asked me about work, my church, and people I knew. I did not give them any new names. I only talked about the people whom they mentioned specifically and tried not to give them any new information. One was the pastor and another person was a close friend whom I met at the international church. I always talked about these relationships in the context of our shared international church. When they finished asking me questions, I asked them why I was there and what I did to deserve all this, but they didn't give me any answers. I asked them if I could add something to what I had previously said, and they allowed me to do so. I said, "I know that you think that I am involved in politics, but you are wrong. You will never find anything to support this. I am a businessman, and you should verify my qualifications and the legitimacy of my business. I also believe in Jesus, and because He has changed my life, I speak about Jesus to anyone who would like to know who He is. He died for my sins, and I have surrendered my whole life to Him." They had no response and sent me back to the prison.

I went back to my prison cell and started to pray again. I felt very weak and said to the Lord, "Oh, God, how long will this go on? I need You so much. I don't know how to survive here without You!" The Lord answered my prayer with peace in my heart, and I continued to pray. Often I prayed for hours at a time, and I also prayed in tongues when I didn't know what to pray anymore.

The Holy Spirit started to speak to my heart—it was as if God was saying that He allowed me to be there. I knew that the Lord wanted to spend some time with me and talk to me. I was in such a busy season, and it looked like life would just get busier in the future. In the cell, all the work was gone, and I had time to listen to God's voice. He started to reveal sin in my life of which I wasn't aware. He revealed it so clearly that it was like watching myself in a movie. I wept over the sin that the Lord showed me and asked him to cleanse me with His blood. This was such a precious time.

Then He started to speak to me about the future and our ministry. I wanted to remember these precious words and prophecies about my life, but I didn't have a pen or paper. So I decided to assign a letter to each word or prophecy, and I repeated letters every day in my mind and prayed through them to keep them in my heart. I prayed about all these things day after day. On the sixth day, I was taken out of my cell again for the next interrogation. This time I was allowed to walk through the prison area without a blindfold. I couldn't believe what I saw. People were chained around their necks, hands, and feet. Two men were carrying another man because his feet were broken. I saw that these people were treated very differently than I was.

Before we exited the prison, I was blindfolded and handcuffed and taken back to the security office where I expected to be interrogated again. This time they did not remove the blindfold or handcuffs. When I heard voices and people approaching me, I expected to be tortured. I prayed, "Lord, please, help me and make me strong in You. I can do nothing, and I am afraid without You, but with You I can endure it. Please, help me to be faithful to You and to be a witness for You in every situation." They started to interrogate me, and after a while I was allowed to see and released from the handcuffs. They never tortured me at all. In fact, I got my Bible back, and I was allowed to take it to my cell later on.

11

THE WORD

During the first six days of my imprisonment, I learned how to enjoy Jesus through prayer and meditating on the Bible verses that I knew by heart. It was a great experience and showed me the importance of learning Scripture by heart. I also sang many songs that I knew by heart. Now that I had a Bible, I devoured it like never before. I read through the whole Bible several times and received life as I enjoyed fellowship with God through His Word. I started to understand the stories that I had read from Russia and China where people were so hungry to read God's word, but could not easily get it. We don't know what we have in this beautiful treasure of the word of God until it is taken from us.

> We don't know what we have in this beautiful treasure of the word of God until it is taken from us.

I could barely keep up with all of the things God spoke to me and didn't want to forget anything. I began pulling little strings from the mat in my cell to use them as bookmarks. I ended up having more than 120 strings in my Bible, and I looked at them daily to remember what God told me through the different verses. He often spoke to me through the Psalms and the Proverbs. Many psalms start with complaints, struggles, and a

description of the psalm writer's circumstance at the moment. He then either cries out to the Lord or weeps and asks the Lord to intervene. Nearly every time, the writer finishes the psalm with thanksgiving and worship, acknowledging God's faithfulness and greatness in every situation.

Psalm 28:2,6–7

Hear the voice of my pleas for mercy, when I cry to you for help,
when I lift up my hands toward your most holy sanctuary.
Blessed be the LORD! For he has heard the voice of my pleas for mercy.
The LORD is my strength and my shield; in him my heart trusts,
and I am helped; my heart exults, and with my song I give thanks to him.

Psalm 22:5

To you they cried and were rescued;
in you they trusted and were not put to shame.

Psalm 22:8

He trusts in the LORD; let him deliver him;
let him rescue him, for he delights in him!

Psalm 22:11, 19

Be not far from me, for trouble is near, and there is none to help.
But you, O LORD, do not be far off! O you my help,
come quickly to my aid!

Psalm 116:1–15

I love the LORD, because he has heard my voice and my pleas for mercy.
Because he inclined his ear to me,
therefore I will call on him as long as I live.
The snares of death encompassed me; the pangs of Sheol laid hold on me;
I suffered distress and anguish.
Then I called on the name of the LORD: "O LORD, I pray,
deliver my soul!"
Gracious is the LORD, and righteous; our God is merciful.
The LORD preserves the simple; when I was brought low, he saved me.

Return, O my soul, to your rest; for the LORD has dealt
bountifully with you.
For you have delivered my soul from death, my eyes from tears,
my feet from stumbling;
I will walk before the LORD in the land of the living.
I believed, even when I spoke: "I am greatly afflicted";
I said in my alarm, "All mankind are liars."
What shall I render to the LORD for all his benefits to me?
I will lift up the cup of salvation and call on the name of the LORD,
I will pay my vows to the LORD in the presence of all his people.
Precious in the sight of the LORD is the death of his saints.

One time while reading through the book of Acts, I was touched by the story of Paul and Silas in prison. As they worshipped, God opened the prison door, and they were free. I said to the Lord, "I know that You are the same God and that You can do exactly the same thing for me that You did for Paul and Silas. What a great testimony it would be if tomorrow I were to walk on the streets of our city. All the security police would know that Jesus is the Truth, and He is the One who delivered me from prison. And at the same time I would be free and could see my family." My heart's desire was for God to be glorified, but I also wanted to be free.

I started to daydream about how wonderful it would be to embrace my wife and my kids and to surprise them with a knock at the door and a testimony that Jesus set me free. I prayed about this for a long time and asked the Lord for His will to be done. On one hand, I had faith that the Lord Jesus could do it. On the other hand, I also knew that many believers were bringing glory to Jesus from prison.

A month before I was taken to prison, I preached a sermon on Hebrews 11 and 12, and in this moment, my own words came back to me. Jesus was glorified through all the miracles and signs and wonders the Holy Spirit did through His servants. Jesus was also glorified through all those who were in prison, those who were tortured, and those who laid down their lives for Him. My main point was that Jesus could be glorified both through signs and wonders and through suffering in His name. I resolved in my heart to hope in the One who could miraculously release me or allow me to stay in prison for the glory of His name. That night, God honored my resolution.

In the middle of the night, I was awakened by a very loud noise. I immediately looked at the prison door to see if it was open, but the door was still closed and locked. I thought that I was dreaming and went back to sleep. In the morning when I woke up, I could see the sky through a 15–20 centimeter crack in the ceiling, and when I went to the bathroom, I discovered that several ceramic stones had fallen on the floor. These tiles probably had caused the noise I had heard in the night. I thought there must have been an earthquake during the night, but the guards confirmed the next morning that mine was the only cell that had been damaged. They put me into a new cell. While the

> Jesus could be glorified both through signs and wonders and through suffering in His name.

crack wasn't big enough for me to escape, God confirmed His presence with me and released faith, comfort, and courage in my heart. He said, "See, I am able to open prison doors today just as I did for Paul and Silas. But I haven't finished my work with you yet. I want to continue to spend time with you and teach you more things."

At this point, I was still fasting from all food and only drinking water. Physically, I was strong and able to enjoy the Lord's presence. Emotionally, I felt weak at times and cried before the Lord, asking Him to protect my family and the faith of my children who were thirteen and eleven years old at the time. I did not want them to doubt God's love for us, nor did I want their faith to be shaken.

After I had been in prison for ten days, my wife found out where I was, and she was able to drop off food and clothes at the security office. From that point on, I received fruits and vegetables and clean clothes every few days. I started to eat fruits and vegetables and continued with this "Daniel fast" until I was released. Even though I lost about fifteen kilograms, I was physically very strong until the end.

Except for the three times I was questioned, the time one guard broke the rules to talk to me, and my last night in a group cell, it was the Lord and I alone together for fifty-eight days and nights. Although the time in prison was exceedingly difficult, I experienced a kind of intimacy with Jesus that I had never previously known. His presence and His voice were more obvious and clear than they had ever been before.

12

DAILY ROUTINE

My primary worry in prison was that this situation would negatively impact my children's faith in God, but a close second was that I would be in this prison cell, separated from my family, for years. I often spent time in prayer regarding these fears. Sometimes peace came within a few minutes, and sometimes I had to pray for an hour or more. When peace and joy would come, I knew the Lord would give me the strength I would need to endure this trial, even if it lasted for years.

When I got my Bible on the sixth day, I felt the need for a daily routine since it seemed like I might be there awhile. Both of the windows in my cell had six bars that created something like little compartments between the bars. I used the little packets of sugar and salt from the guards to track the days and weeks. In one window, I moved the sugar packets from one compartment to the next to track the number of days I had been in prison. In the other window, I used the salt packets to count the weeks. This helped me know exactly how many days I was in prison and kept me oriented to the date and day of the week. I turned forty-five on my thirty-seventh day in prison.

My first cell was very disorienting because a light was on 24 hours a day. After the earthquake, my new cell had a light bulb that I unscrewed to have a more normal day and night rhythm. I usually went to bed a few hours after sunset and woke up with the sunrise. I started the day by drinking my water and doing pushups. In the beginning, I could only do a few, but by the end of my time in prison, I did twenty or more at a time, three or four times a day. This helped me to keep my body in good shape. Next, I read about twenty psalms loudly out the window. This helped me to hear the Word as opposed to only reading it quietly. Even though probably no one else understood it, it was my daily breakfast. After this, I went into the bathroom and worshipped the Lord. I sang dozens of hymns that I remembered from my childhood and some newer songs as well. During the time of worship, I exercised by stepping up and down on the hard plastic basin that was supposed to be used for washing my clothes. After my exercise, I took a shower and went back to my cell to memorize Scripture. I memorized eight to ten verses per day. After fifty-eight days, I had memorized the whole book of James and all but the last chapter of Romans. Every day I would repeat all the verses I learned previously and add new ones. At the beginning it only took a few minutes. By the end, I was spending a couple of hours on Scripture memorization every day. The Lord made His word alive to me and often taught me about verses that I hadn't previously understood. After this, I went back to the bathroom and interceded for my family, parents, relatives, neighbors, the work in our country, my fellow workers, and for all my other relationships. During the intercession time, I exercised on the plastic basin again.

After intercession, I went back to my room and systematically read the Bible. I enjoyed the time I had to simply read the Word and listen to the Holy Spirit speak to me. Next, I went back to the bathroom to intercede for all the nations of the world, especially for the Muslim nations. I really felt that the Holy Spirit gave me a new and fresh burden to pray and intercede for them. Again, I exercised in the same way on the basin at the same time. Usually by this time, the day was over, and it was dark.

I did not have a watch, but I imagine my day went something like this:

06:30
Wake up with the sunrise

06:40
Wash my face and drink water
(or later some fruit juice that I received from my wife)

07:00
Read twenty psalms aloud and pray through/with them

09:00

Worship the Lord with songs and exercise in the bathroom

12:00

Memorize Scripture

15:00

Intercede for all my friends and family and exercise in the bathroom

17:00

Read the Bible systematically

19:00

Intercede for the nations and exercise at the same time in the bathroom

21:30

Go to bed

13

VISITORS

On the eighteenth day, I was taken out of my cell again to what I assumed to be another time of questioning, but instead of going to the security office, we went to another room in the prison. When they opened the door, I saw my wife Sara and my two children with the consul. I was very surprised. I took my two kids in my arms and gave my wife a hug. We spoke a little bit, and I enjoyed the presence of my family with me. My son Ezekiel said to me, "Father, I am proud that you are here. You are here because of Jesus, and I am proud of you." My daughter Lea couldn't talk much because she was too emotional, but it seemed that she was doing fine as well, just very much in need of a visit with her father. She put on her most beautiful clothes, a little bit of make-up, and her favorite perfume. It was especially sweet to smell Lea's perfume on my shirt for the next few days in the cell. We were allowed to visit for about thirty minutes, and we also received some information from security. We found out they would allow my family to visit me about every twenty days, and that after a total of fifty days in prison, they would either have to take me to court, release me, or ask for another period of fifty days for the investigation process. During the thirty-minute visits, we were not allowed to talk about topics related to my imprisonment, and Sara and I were only allowed to speak in English. However, they allowed the children and me to talk with each other in our mother tongue. We therefore planned to share our thoughts for the next visit through our kids in our mother tongue that no one else could understand.

It was great to know that my wife and kids were doing fine and that the Lord was answering my prayers for their well-being and their faith. I felt a deep love coming from Sara and the children towards me, and this gave me much strength to endure. Although I was very happy to see my family, it was much harder to go back to my cell and face reality again. I just wept, thanking the Lord for allowing me to see my family and also offering back to Him my longing to see them more often and to be reunited with them again. From my cell I could hear the airplanes flying over me, and sometimes I was comforted by the thought that some day, I would leave the country as a free man and be together with my family.

Once during my daily routine, I asked the Lord to speak specifically to me. I waited quietly and asked the Lord to give me a Bible verse or a page number in my Bible. He gave me Revelation 7:14, page 968 on which I found Proverbs 21:21, and 2 Chronicles 7:1–4.

Revelation 7:14 "*. . . These are the ones coming out of the great tribulation. They have washed their robes and made them white in the blood of the Lamb.*"

Proverbs 21:21 "*Whoever pursues righteousness and kindness will find life, righteousness, and honor.*"

2 Chronicles 7:1–4 "*As soon as Solomon finished his prayer, fire came down from heaven and consumed the burnt offering and the sacrifices, and the glory of the* Lord *filled the temple. And the priests could not enter the house of the* Lord, *because the glory of the* Lord *filled the* Lord's *house. When all the people of Israel saw the fire come down and the glory of the* Lord *on the temple, they bowed down with their faces to the ground on the pavement and worshiped and gave thanks to the* Lord, *saying, 'For he is good, for his steadfast love endures forever.' Then the king and all the people offered sacrifice before the* Lord.*"

The Spirit gave me clarity on the meaning of the combination of these verses for this time. In the beginning of my time in prison, He had cleansed my heart by revealing my sin, and now He knew that I wanted to be with Him and that I was eager to pursue righteousness with all my heart. I felt His desire to bless me with His love, to prosper me in His kingdom, and to honor His holy name more than ever before. Through the last Bible verse, I felt that the Lord wanted to refill me with the power of the Holy Spirit and that I should be filled in the way He filled the temple of Solomon.

The "Eid al Kabir," the largest and most important feast for Muslims during the year, was approaching, and the Lord told me that I should not fast on that day but celebrate instead. I should celebrate the feast not for their religious reason, but I should celebrate the refilling of my life with the Holy Spirit. I then told the guards that I would not fast on that day, and they brought me meat to eat from the holiday celebration. I celebrated that day in my cell and enjoyed the delicious meat.

As usual, I went into the bathroom to worship the Lord, but this time the Holy Spirit filled the bathroom with His presence in a way that I had never experienced before in my life. I felt the presence of God so clearly that I started to weep, cry, laugh, sing, worship, and praise the Lord in tongues. It was such a powerful experience that I stayed in there for hours just to enjoy God's presence in my life. I knew that the guards outside must have heard my singing and praying, but I didn't care. I just wanted to be close to Jesus and experience His love and His presence.

In the coming days, the Lord guided me into deeper intercession, and He started to give me words of knowledge for the guards. The next time a guard came to my window to give me some tea, I heard the name Zeinab in my heart. I asked him if the name Zeinab meant anything to him. Surprised, he said, "Yes, that is my wife's name." I told him that the Lord had spoken to me about her and that He would like to bless them with a baby. Now he really was surprised and said, "She is only one month pregnant, and I am the only other person who knows. Who told you about this?" I told him that God had revealed it to me and that I would like to pray for him that Jesus would show them the truth of God and bless them. He was very willing to accept this, and I prayed with him for the blessing of God, in the name of Jesus, to be upon him, his wife, and his future baby. Other experiences similar to this one encouraged me to see that the Lord enables us to share Jesus wherever we are, even in prison.

The second time my family visited, I knew in advance, so I was able to shave my face and wear clean clothes. God had put several things on my heart to share with my wife. God gave me some Bible verses for my family.

Proverbs 12:4 "*An excellent wife is the crown of her husband.*"

Psalm 119:9 "*How can a young man keep his way pure? By guarding it according to your word.*"

I also had some practical things to share with my wife. For instance, I wanted her to sell our car because security could steal it otherwise.

I wanted to express my deepest love and appreciation to my wife and show her how proud and thankful I was. I planned to give her a real kiss even if all the guards and the security people present would be embarrassed because such a thing never happened publicly in their culture. But I felt that showing my wife my deepest commitment to her was more important than following cultural rules.

When the time came and I was taken out of my cell to meet with my family, I was prepared. When I saw them, I greeted my wife with a real kiss and gave kisses and hugs to my children. After we sat down, my countenance became serious, and I sat up straight. I said in English loudly so that the guards could hear, "If I am the reason that our educational institution is being shut down, they should send me and my family out of the country. I am willing to go now." Then I relaxed back into my chair and started to share the things I had prepared to share with my family. We spent time together and the kids shared with me what they were doing in school and at home. We also prayed for each other and blessed each other and prayed for the security guards in their presence.

> Love is more important than anything else. It overcomes cultural differences if it is done with a full and pure heart.

After I was released, I found out that Sara and the kids had an elaborate plan to ask me some important questions during our second visit. Since the guards let the kids and me speak in our mother tongue at our last visit, Ezekiel was ready to do all the talking, but Lea had composed a song with the questions just in case they stopped Ezekiel from speaking. When I said to the guards that I was ready to leave the country, I answered the very questions that Sara and the kids had planned to ask me. It was the Holy Spirit speaking through me to confirm the change in our family's plan from trying to stay in the country to being willing to leave.

When the time came to an end, we prayed with each other and said goodbye. This was a very emotional moment, but we also felt that God was with all of us.

When the guard took me back to my cell he said, "I am not married yet, but I hope to get married next year. There is so much love in your family. I would like to have such a family one day." It was not just the kiss I gave to my wife that left an impression on him. It was surely the way we spoke and treated each other. It seemed like the kiss made a positive impression on him when I had expected the opposite. When he told me this, I felt convinced that love is more important than anything else. It overcomes cultural differences if it is done with a full and pure heart. Love touches people of every culture.

After the guard locked me back up in my cell, I cried for a while because I missed my family very much. I was also thankful to God for His protection of all of them.

Before the third time my family visited, a friendly security man told me the day and time they would come. As I prepared for our visit, I felt that we should ask our friends and prayer networks to pray and fast for three days for my release. The security guards were much friendlier to us this time, and they even allowed us to speak in our mother tongue. We all hoped that this was a good sign, but we didn't know for sure. We agreed to start a three-day fast on my fifty-sixth day of imprisonment.

14

AN ENDING AND
A BEGINNING

On the second day of our fast, the guard came to me in the morning and said, "Today you will be released and deported." I thought that he was joking and didn't really believe him. He insisted that I should prepare my things and get ready to leave. With some excitement, I packed my things, and indeed, an hour later they opened the door and took me out of my cell. After about twenty minutes of waiting outside, they asked me to go back into the cell because the car had not come yet. I was not sure whether they were playing games with me, or the car was really just late. An hour later, they took me out again, and I was taken by the main security man in his personal car out of the prison. He was very friendly this time and told me that we were going to the other side of town to do some paperwork, and then I would be deported. I asked him what would happen to my family since they would need my exit visa as the head of the household in order to apply for exit visas for themselves. The Lord touched his heart, and he allowed me to use his personal phone to call my wife and tell her that we should meet on the other side of the town at the police station. When I finally reached her, she couldn't believe that I was on the phone. She had just finished a meeting with people from our embassy and our lawyer to discuss the next steps. When they heard my voice on the phone, they realized that security had changed their plan, and the lawyer and my wife went immediately to the police station.

I arrived before they did and was waiting to see what would happen. Security officers brought the 130 MP3 players into the room and started to throw them on the floor. About twenty-five policemen started to examine and investigate them. I saw that I was not being released. Now I would be tried, and the MP3 players would serve as evidence against me. My hope was that they would leave the players so that my wife and the lawyer could take them away when they came. About ten minutes later, my wife and the lawyer arrived and saw all these players on the floor. Without saying much, they left the room again. A couple minutes later, the lawyer's assistant came into the room, collected all the players and left the room with them. A few moments later my wife showed up and said to me in our language, "If they ask you where these players are, just tell them that you don't know."

Then I was taken out of the room to another prison. This time, I was in the same room with about fifty different people. Some were murderers and thieves, and there were even some small children who had stolen little things from the market because they were hungry.

This was the first time I had access to a pen and paper, so I wrote all the things down the Lord had spoken to me in prison so that I would not forget them. Nothing was provided for the prisoners here. All the food and clothes had to be provided by friends or family. Sara brought me a mattress and a little exercise mat so that I could sleep.

I discovered that most of the people had a phone with them even though having a phone was officially forbidden. I asked my wife to bring a phone with her so that we could stay in contact. When she tried to give it to me, the guard wouldn't let her. I offered him the exercise mat that my wife had brought me, and then he allowed me to take the phone into the cell. This is probably how all the others were able to get their phones as well. I was extremely happy to have a phone, and I called some of our family members as soon as I could.

The next day most of the fifty people were taken to court to receive their judgment. The lawyer came to see me early in the morning and told me that he would discover which of the seventeen judges had my file so that he could meet him in advance. Around eleven a.m., he came back and told me that everything should be all right and that he was able to come to an agreement with the judge. When I was brought into the court hall, I found the judge, the lawyer, and a few witnesses there. The judge was listening to the person who brought the accusations against me. To my surprise they only accused me of being in the country illegally. Since my visa had expired three months ago, this was the truth. My visa had expired because security had not accepted the visa renewal application. Finally the judge asked me if this was true, and I told him that it was. He judged me with a small fine, and I had to pay a $200 fee. No other charges against me were mentioned. Only later at the airport did I learn that they had two files against me accusing me of much more significant offenses that could have resulted in many years of prison. I praise the Lord that He saved me like this. Before I was taken to the airport, I spent several hours at the police station. They gave me back my bag, which enabled me to buy some meat for myself and for the guards to celebrate my release. I was then taken to the airport at 11 p.m. to fly out. My family followed the next day so that Lea could finish her school camping trip as planned.

The kingdom of God often grows through troubling and challenging times. Countries that face war, ethnic cleansing*, natural disasters, or persecution of believers often experience a tremendous growth of the kingdom of God. On the other hand, we know of cases where heavy persecution has destroyed part of the church. While we don't want to glorify persecution or the atrocities of war and genocide* at all, the reality is that often many people turn to the Lord Jesus because of them. Tertullian, one of the church fathers said, "The blood of the believers is the seed of the church."

After my release, more than two hundred Christian foreign workers had to leave the country. It is clear that the government decided to cleanse the country from all Christian activity. They also increased the persecution of local Christians. Some of them have been interrogated, tortured, and stripped of their citizenship. In several areas of the country, war rages on, creating tens of thousands of refugees who are now living in camps in neighboring countries.

During our relatively short time in the country, we saw an increase in the number of people from certain tribes turn to Christ. After the expulsion of all the Christian workers, we have heard about a greater openness for the gospel in unreached tribes within the borders of the country itself and in refugee camps outside the border in neighboring countries. A recent conference to equip local believers to reach out to Muslims in the refugee camps has revealed a great openness to the gospel due to the suffering which caused them to be in the camps in the first place. We pray and expect to see a great harvest for the glory of Jesus.

15

LESSONS LEARNED

1. Living your life for God is the most adventurous and exciting thing one can do with his life no matter where in the world one lives. You don't have to go overseas to daily submit your life to God and ask Him to lead you to do the works He has prepared in advance for you to do.

2. While most people, including myself, would not have been surprised if my children had reacted with ill feelings toward God, the opposite happened! My children's faith grew during this difficult season.

3. It is not clear whether my prison experience was a trial, a temptation, or a mix of both. What I do know is that the Lord will never allow us to be tempted beyond what we can bear, and He provides the power we need when we are weak during trials.

4. We must pursue an intimate relationship with Jesus. That intimacy is the source of all fruit in our lives, whether the fruit is external in the form of ministry or internal in the form of sanctification.

5. Whoever seeks to live a holy life before God will be persecuted. There are different kinds of persecution such as the loss of a good reputation, the loss of possessions, prison, torture, and death. The Lord knows which kind of persecution to allow for each person so that his character is transformed, and Jesus is honored.

6. The way that the body of Christ came together to support my family and me during this trial made a huge difference in our ability to persevere in faith. We received support from local believers, from expatriate believers from different denominations and organizations in our host country, and from believers all over the world.

7. During difficult trials, we must never let discouragement or hopelessness destroy our faith. In our weakness we must turn to Jesus for strength to persevere. My wife, kids, and I each had several moments during this time when we had to choose faith and resist the temptation to give up.

8. In this world we can be stripped of everything—our homes, our work, and even our spouse and children. We must learn to be fully satisfied with Jesus alone because He is the only One who cannot be taken away. When I was in prison, I had nothing but Jesus, and in the midst of an intense longing for my wife and kids, His sweet presence was enough to endure this trial.

9. As we follow the Lord radically, we will be an aroma of death and look foolish to the world. To those who know Him, however, we are the fragrance of life and spur them on to follow our example in living a life completely abandoned for Christ. While some people expressed their disapproval of my choices, several people have told me that watching my family give up everything for Jesus inspired them to follow Jesus more passionately than ever before.

10. Look for the humor in your life no matter how intense or difficult the situation is. We can keep a sense of humor and be joyful in any situation. For example, during one of our thirty-minute visits as a family, we laughed about the fact that while I was going to spend the Eid (a local holiday) in prison, Sara and the kids were planning to go to the nicest hotel in town.

11. Even though we were forced by security to leave our host country, it was God who allowed it to happen because He is the One who numbers our days. Count each day in your host culture as a gift from God and use it wisely because you don't know how much time God will give you there. Several people who were expelled from our host country expressed regret that they did not share Jesus enough during the time that they were allowed to be there. For those of us who are advancing the kingdom in our own cultures, we are also not guaranteed the number of days that we have in our schools, work places, caring for our children, or living next to our neighbors. We must all use our time wisely and share the good news of our King Jesus at every opportunity so that we do not have any regrets.

12. Know your identity in your host country and be able to phrase it simply in one or two sentences. You can respond to almost all questions people have of you with this prepared statement. Be sure to include your identity

as a follower of Jesus. The statement that I repeated over and over again was, "I am a businessman who loves Jesus, and I talk to people about Him whenever I can."

13. While I was in prison, God spoke to me about the importance of having a daily family devotional. Sara was very grateful that this had been our family habit for many years and that I had spent a lot of time talking with the kids about persecution in general, about my arrests, and the possibility of prison in the future. The kids were more prepared because of these kinds of conversations that had happened often during our family devotional time. While I was in prison, God gave me a fresh outline for our devotional times based on Ecclesiastes 9:7–10 and Exodus 20:12. I have outlined our family devotional in Appendix 1 and would invite you to read it and use it for your own if you would like.

Jesus was faithful, is faithful, and is going to remain faithful. If we trust Him in all situations, we will never be disappointed.

16

SARA'S STORY

Before sharing my personal experience about Daniel's imprisonment, you need to understand a part of my history and my journey with the Lord. The reason that I could stand during the bittersweet and challenging fifty-eight days of his imprisonment was not because I was emotionally strong, nor did I have a spirit of adventure—it was actually the opposite! Before I got married, my team leader's wife, who mentored me into marriage and ministry and knew me well, said to me, "Sara, you have a solid walk with the Lord, and physically you are strong and do not need much rest, so you can achieve many things, more than many others. But for the ministry that you have ahead of you, you must become stronger emotionally." This was the first time in my life that I had received such a strong exhortation. Though it was hard to hear, I knew she was right. I was aware on some level that I needed to grow in this area, but at that moment, I saw how important this issue was and that I desperately needed the Lord to do this work in me.

Not long after we arrived on our first field of service as a married couple, our team received security threats, and Daniel received the first of several personal death threats. With a husband gifted in evangelism, security situations would become a normal part of our apostolic lifestyle. Over time, these threats proved to be a great challenge for me and forced me to deal with my emotional weakness. I often struggled with the fear of losing my husband, and I played out many "what if . . ." scenarios in my mind. I would lose sleep and my appetite. I would often ask the Lord, "How can I withstand this and draw strength from You?" He usually invited me to sit at His feet.

Each time I had a choice to give into fear or trust in the Lord. By His awesome grace, I overcame my fear and continued to trust Him more and more. I also learned to share my burdens openly with Daniel so that we could pray together.

The evening that Daniel was arrested the second time in our second country of ministry, it took us totally by surprise. We had told our good friends that morning over breakfast that we believed God was giving us another season of ministry in this country, and we had shared some of our personal plans, dreams, and hopes with them. Since the men who took him were in plain clothes, we were not sure if they were kidnappers or from security. I was really relieved when he was allowed to call and tell me that he was with security, and I felt very grateful when he was released to spend the night with us at home. This gave us a chance to pray together, make decisions, and sharpen our contingency plans.

During that season, I experienced an intense spiritual battle in a way I hadn't before. With each prayer call from the nearby mosque, I felt a dark cloud come on me like big crows wanting to nest in my mind. I sought out the help of a co-worker in our town who loved Jesus and who had challenged me in the past to grow in my walk with the Lord. Over the coming six months as Daniel dealt with security, she and I regularly spent time together sharing and praying. During this time, I also started to spend more time in the Word and in personal worship. It was a wonderful season during which the Lord prepared me for what was to come.

God also orchestrated an opportunity for me to teach in a local primary school. It was a private school, and most of my young students were the children of government and security officials. I was under a lot of scrutiny as there were security cameras in each classroom. During that year, I grew in courage to answer boldly for what I believe and what I do. I had to do it all by myself since Daniel could not solve the problems for me.

It actually didn't come as a total surprise to me when Daniel was suddenly taken one evening in October 2012. Ever since we had moved into this new neighborhood across the river, it seemed like we were being watched more by security. And there was one neighbor who seemed to have something against us as he was not friendly and would sometimes point at our house from the street as he talked with other people. The spiritual climate in our neighborhood and our house felt heavy and dark. We also noticed an increase in the number of visits from security at our educational center. At the time, I wondered if these were distractions from the enemy to make us tired, but I also wondered if something more serious was coming.

Over the years, I have learned to regularly review our contingency plans and adjust them if necessary. I also have a packing list ready so I don't have to think too much when the unexpected happens. Since I sensed something might be coming, I asked Daniel to remind me of all passwords and review important information about our bank accounts and insurance. We also reviewed our identity statement. I have come to refer to this as a "pre-event stress reliever."

The evening that Daniel was arrested and imprisoned was the beginning of a race with an uncertain finish line. First, I talked to my kids, and we prayed for Daniel's protection and for peace for all of us. Then I informed specific co-workers and the leaders of our sending organization*. Later in the evening, I informed our embassy, local friends in high positions, our families back home, and my prayer partner in town. I hid our computers, hard drives, some of our books, and Daniel's cell phone in creative places like the washing machine under dirty clothes, the freezer under some food, the oven, and in the chicken coop. Nothing was found the next day when they came to search our house.

Around the kid's bedtime, someone knocked on our door. We thought security had come to search our house. Instead, a branch manager from one of the educational centers had come for a meeting that he and Daniel had scheduled a few weeks prior. I told him what was going on, and his response was, "Sara, unless Daniel is coming home tonight, I'm not going to leave you and the kids alone." This colleague (whose family was back in Europe) felt it was his duty to protect us as a family, to help and advise us when needed, and to arrange things so that the kids and I would not have to be alone. From that day on, there was always a man with us in the house overnight. Most of the time it was "Luemel," who was known by local people* as my younger brother because we were from the same home country, and he lived with us. We were incredibly blessed to have him with us for meal times and for spending time with the kids when I had to follow up on so many newfound responsibilities due to the absence of my husband.

A few days later, one of my friends, who was from an important government family and who had been trying to gather information for us, told me that our situation was very serious and that Daniel might be in prison for longer than a few days or weeks or maybe even years. The kids asked me so many "if" and "when" questions. I wanted to be realistic with them and at the same time, protect them from information that could have been burdensome. When we talked through the possibility of Daniel being detained for years, I assured them that unless the government forced the three of us to leave, we would stay. "I will find a job, and we will move to a small apartment close to your school. We will live as normally as possible and see dad as often as they will allow." This conversation seemed to help the kids (and me too).

There were a few other important decisions we made right at the beginning in order to run the unknown race ahead of us well.

- We kept the normal family schedule—sharing mealtimes together, having devotions before going to bed, going to the international church on Friday, and going out to lunch afterwards.
- We wanted to continue eating healthy and sleeping well.
- We drafted a simple statement for the kids so that they would be prepared and confident to answer questions from any person (even if that meant saying "That's a question you should ask my mom.")
- We made it a priority to deal with feelings of fear, anger, sadness, etc. and would not downplay or ignore them.
- We adapted our apartment to the situation. (We shared the bedroom, and the children's room was for packing and visitors.)
- We communicated and kept boundaries. Our need to spend relaxed time together was greater than our need to hang out with others.
- We kept making plans for activities and fun.
- I would meet regularly with my co-worker friend in town to share openly and pray through all the deep emotions that can surface in such circumstances.

The temptation was extremely great to just shut down all of our emotions and move into a state of numbness. The children and I kept praying together for Daniel and for ourselves that the Lord might give each one of us grace to live fully and not let our hearts become hard or bitter. We tried to stay emotionally connected with Daniel by journaling and writing him letters, not knowing if he would ever see them. In addition, I kept a notebook to keep the facts in order to be able to track the steps and initiatives we took. These letters were really precious to Daniel when he received them after his release.

Another turning point for the kids in dealing with fear, sadness, confusion, anger, and all the normal feelings in such circumstances was a letter to them from our close friend, Uncle Jack. The words were indeed from the Lord and sank deep into the children's confused hearts. Uncle Jack and Auntie Janice cared so passionately for us that they wrote in one of their prayer letters that they loved my children as much as they loved their own. Ezekiel and Lea knew that Uncle Jack and Auntie Janice would not say such a thing lightly. They felt very affirmed, loved, and appreciated!

For me, a letter they sent out requesting prayer on our behalf was an encouraging exhortation and helped me to overcome some of my own questions and doubts about whether or not we should be doing more for Daniel to be released. Their letter follows:

> Over two weeks ago, a very good friend and colleague was arrested by security police, and there has been minimal contact. The wife is still unable to see her husband after two long weeks. Events like these help us remember and pray through our priorities. We must approach these situations with the long term view in mind.
>
> Emotionally this is very hard to do. When we are in the middle of the situation our priority naturally shifts to the welfare (and in our minds this means the release) of our loved one.
>
> I am not so sure God's priority ever shifts. There are several things more important than the health and comfort and release of the incarcerated. Let me list some of them:
>
> 1) The Glory of God
>
> It is informative how central prison is to the plan of God. Joseph, Jeremiah, John the Baptist, James, Peter, Paul—and many others in Scripture and history—all testify to God being glorified in confinement. We remind ourselves with Joseph that it is not about us, and that what "man intended for evil, God intended for good." We encourage ourselves in the Pauline Epistles and forget that many of them were written from prison repose.

2) The Credibility of the Gospel

When followers of Jesus go to prison, it puts the gospel on display. Do we live what we preach?

Do we believe what we say? Is God enough? Is Jesus our strong tower? Is the Holy Spirit a comfort? Are these platitudes of the insulated or are they truths burned into our souls by trial?

When missionaries suffer well, it sends a message to indigenous believers (who suffer much more than we do) that Jesus is indeed worth suffering for and that we are in solidarity with their difficulty.

Suffering well also is a witness to our tormentors. Athanasius insisted that one of the proofs of the resurrection was the joy with which women and children faced physical abuse and death.

3) The Character of the Prisoner and His Family

God works in us when we are stripped down, confined, abused, and mistreated. There is a joy in the fellowship of his sufferings. The seldom experienced (for we fear the process) reward of prison and persecution is unimaginable intimacy with Jesus—which delights our soul. Tales from the released surprise us as they pine for the good old days of the cement cell because Jesus' presence was unmitigated and pristine. God also works in the hearts of spouses and children in these admittedly painful times—if we let Him.

All the above are more important than the health and release of the captive. This is not callous, this is Christ. It is not about us and it is not about our security. Helen Keller—who knew much about being confined—said, "Security is mostly a superstition. It does not exist in nature,

Suffering well also is a witness to our tormentors.

nor do children of men as a whole experience it. Avoiding danger is no safer in the long run than outright exposure. Life is either a daring adventure, or nothing."

If we take the short view, we move heaven and earth to see our loved one released. In one sense this is admirable. In another sense, it can be self-serving. When I was arrested some years ago,

I appreciated the efforts of those working to free me—but I would have been livid if they pursued my freedom in such a way that affected my longevity in the land (and among the people) I have been called to serve and die for if necessary. The long-term view undergirds the prisoner in his lonely cell. He does not want a frantic, panicked effort to release him. He wants to stay in the country after his release. He does not want external voices to shame the local authorities or force his expulsion—that can be a fate more cruel than lonely prison days.

Those who speak to us from prison say, "We are fine. Jesus is real. We are being upheld by the Holy Spirit and are in sweet communion with the Father. Don't worry about us. Don't panic. Don't rush the process. We are improving our language skills; we have plenty of time to pray. We are witnessing to our captors. We appreciate your efforts—for the soul of man is destined to be free—but we beg of you: proceed slowly and respectfully, for our greatest desire is for Jesus to be glorified in the process and to continue exalting Him in this beloved land (if at all possible) even after our release. So if we have to sit here a few extra weeks or months, so be it."

Time is on the side of the righteous. Let's remember who really is in prison after all, and let's take the long-term view, let's endure what we must that they may be set free.

And what of the children of the imprisoned? If you are interested, read the letter I wrote to the children of our dear imprisoned friend—children we love as much as we love our own. It is what I want someone to tell my boys if I ever go back to prison or if we ever are asked to lay down our lives for Jesus.

In constant hope,
Jack and Janice
with John and Josh

Before our first visit with Daniel, I prepared the kids and told them not to be intimidated by harsh and unfriendly security people or an unshaven and surprised dad. I said, "We might not even be able to actually touch dad as he might be kept behind a wire fence or a window." We wanted to communicate to him that we loved and missed him and were very proud of him. We wanted him to know that we were doing well, that many people around the world were praying for him, and that we were working day and night on his case. The four security guards, who sat next to us listening carefully to make sure our conversation did not include details about his case, graciously let the kids speak to their father in their mother tongue. We were very relieved to know that he was truly doing well in light of the circumstances, that he had a Bible with him, and that he had a daily routine including exercise. Daniel released the kids to do things that brought them joy and told them that we would have a long family holiday in a nice place when he was released. Leaving him behind was not easy, but we were assured that he was experiencing the Lord like never before.

From our previous conversations during similar security problems, I had no doubt in my heart that Daniel would want me to pursue his freedom but not at the cost of us having to leave the country, unless the Lord spoke clearly otherwise. This approach complimented our embassy's strategy well. However, one day during the fourth week, I felt doubt rising in my heart about our current course. The question in my heart was, "When would it be right to tell security that we were willing to leave the country if they wanted that from us?" That very morning, I received a prophetic word of exhortation from a prayer warrior telling me that I should let go of our beloved host country and not insist upon holding on. The same day, the leader of our field crisis management team had received a word from God that our mission in the country was fulfilled and that we had the freedom to leave. Since this meant a huge shift in our current approach, I wanted the blessing of our leaders in our home country and of the other few key advisers. We all felt peace about this change in our plan but wanted to confirm it with Daniel. The only way to do that was to wait for the next visit. A week later the consul wanted to meet me and asked if our family would be willing to leave. It was such a wonderful confirmation to me that so many were in agreement about the next steps. The consul accepted our need to wait until our next visit with Daniel even though we did not know for sure when that would happen.

The children and I started praying that the Lord would reveal this plan to Daniel in prison. We greatly rejoiced and praised God for answering our prayers and giving us unity in the Spirit when Daniel pronounced that he was willing to leave. We went straight from the prison to inform the consul that Daniel was ready to leave the country so that the embassy could take the necessary diplomatic steps to advance his release.

Though we were very excited to see him again, this time we knew well the pain that would come after parting with him. Jack encouraged me to "go and shine, laugh and joke with him so that he knows you are all doing well. He really needs to know that." The morning of that visit, I received another word from my close friend who said ". . . go and be his bride." That word articulated my heart's desire for our time together within the thick walls of that dark prison. I wore jewelry and clothes that I knew he liked and fixed my hair to appear like his bride. When I arrived, he kissed me! We had another wonderful visit, encouraging one another, and expressing our love to one another. As we left the prison, we were very thankful for what the Lord was doing in Daniel's life and how the Lord was sustaining him, but we saw that the uncertainty of the future was starting to drain him a little bit.

On our third visit, only one security guard sat with us, and we were allowed to talk in our mother tongue. We tried to answer Daniel's many questions, and we told him what was happening in town, with the business, and the team. He encouraged the kids and asked me to announce three days of prayer and fasting for his release. I was always amazed at the way Daniel was listening to the Spirit and prepared to speak to us. With tears, kisses, hugs, and loving words, we left him again.

Eight days later, at 3:45 a.m. Daniel sat on the airplane and said to me over the phone, "The plane is taking off, I love you!" What a great relief, what a miracle, what a joy! The plane took off without any last minute surprises—that his case was not closed after all, or that they needed another paper, or more fees to be paid. He was free indeed! I couldn't go back to sleep as I had a big day ahead of me. I needed to finish my packing, finish all the paperwork at the kids' school so that they could receive their report cards, and a thousand other small things. A true and faithful friend stayed with me the whole day and helped me with whatever I asked her to do. It was important for me to give the kids a chance to say goodbye to their best friends, so we organized a little farewell party for them at their favorite ice cream place. I had an open house time so that we could say goodbye to our local and foreign friends. It was a beautiful time with lots of tears.

Shortly before midnight, I woke the kids up to go to the airport. The kids went from room to room to say goodbye to our home and we gathered one last time for prayer in our living room together with the friend who had helped me the whole day, Luemel, and the colleague who had said the first evening that he would not leave us alone unless Daniel came back. Then we left our house and our beloved host country and flew to a nearby country. Daniel and Jack picked us up from the airport. We were reunited!

SOME ADVICE FOR THOSE ON THE OUTSIDE

For the spouse or ministry partner

1. Always live with accountability and have someone who is not afraid to speak the truth in love to you regularly. (Ephesians 4:15)
2. Review and adjust on a regular basis your contingency plans, your passwords, and important phone numbers.
3. Have a packing list ready for a "run-bag"* only, and another list in case you are allowed to take a 20kg bag per person.
4. Agree with your spouse/team on how you should approach such a situation. For example, do you want to pursue release as quickly as possible for the prisoner or is it most important to stay in the country?
5. Set your pace and priorities right from the start for your family so that you can persevere for what might be a long season.
6. Let a brother on the field protect you and your family.

For the one who is most likely to be imprisoned

7. Over the years, Daniel had a few close relationships in which he shared his struggles and his dreams. They knew all of the significant things going on in Daniel's life, and they helped him make tough decisions. These men helped me so much while Daniel was in prison because they were able to coach me through this trial and advise me on the many decisions I had to make from a place of confidence in what they thought Daniel would want.

For the sending organization

8. Our sending organization had a crisis management team ready to serve us from day one. They helped us manage all the information, advised us on the many decisions we had to make, prayed for us, and encouraged us.

They also supported our home church* and extended family in our home country.

For the friends, local and far away

9. We were especially encouraged to receive notes, Bible verses, words from the Lord from prayer times, emails, gifts, and offers of help. It is important to remember that the person receiving the different forms of love will be greatly blessed by your kindness but will likely not be able to respond. Sometimes I received over one hundred emails per day, so I could not respond to a great number of those. Also remember that the notes and emails should be worded sensitively as all of our correspondence was under the scrutiny of security.

For the parents of those in prison

10. It made a huge difference that our parents stood with us and supported our decisions. They never expressed doubt or discouraged us about the choices we made. When connecting with them over the phone, they had nothing but affirming and encouraging words for Lea and Ezekiel and in no way gave them the feeling that something was wrong.

17

A LETTER FROM A FRIEND

The following is the letter Jack sent to my family. The Lord used it very powerfully to bring courage to many people, but especially to Ezekiel and Lea.

WHEN DADDY GOES TO PRISON FOR HIS FAITH

October 6, 2012

. . . Yesterday I was thinking about what I would want someone to tell my boys if I was in prison. Here is what I would want them to know:

1) God loves and trusts your dad enough to send him to prison.

In Mark 1:10 the Holy Spirit descends on Jesus. In Mark 1:11 God says, "You are my beloved Son, with you I am well pleased." And then in the very next verse the Spirit drove Jesus into the wilderness—where angels ministered to Him. Your papa is in prison because God loves and trusts him, and God will send angels to minister to your papa.

2) God is completely in control.

In John 19:10 Pilate says to Jesus, "Do you not know that I have authority to release you and authority to crucify you?" Jesus responds (John 19:11): "You would have no authority over me at all unless it had been given you from above . . ." Governments, police, and security, all act real tough and scary, but the only authority they have is because God has given it. In comparison to God—they are powerless. God could destroy or remove them in an instant. God is bigger; God is stronger than any silly, weak security police system. Even when they act so aggressive and intimidating—remember according to God, they are nothing and have no power.

I like to picture David standing over Goliath—who towers over him. Behind Goliath is this massive round shape that makes Goliath look tiny—it is God's big toe! God can crush evil powers without effort and the fact that evil has any power at all is only because ". . . the God of peace . . ." has allowed it (for a time), but ". . . will soon crush Satan under our feet." (Romans 16:20)

3) Bad things happen to good people so God will be glorified.

In John 9:3 Jesus passes by a man who was blind from birth. He was asked whose fault it was. "Jesus answered: 'It was not that this man sinned, or his parents, but that the works of God might be displayed in him.'" Your father has done nothing wrong. In fact, he has done what he is supposed to do: tell everyone everywhere about Jesus! You should be very proud that your father was arrested—it is a sign of his obedience to Jesus' command that we preach Jesus and glorify Him among all peoples. God is going to use this difficult circumstance for His own glory.

We don't know how long prison will last, we don't even know how this will end for us—but that really doesn't matter—what matters is that God gets the glory in how your father acts, reacts, and in what Jesus does. When you pray for your dad, pray that he continues to act, speak, and react in such a way that the works of God are displayed in him.

4) Our God is a God of deliverance.

In Daniel 3:17 three Hebrew young men are to be thrown into the fiery furnace. They tell the king: ". . . He will deliver us . . ." (NIV) They knew that God is always able to deliver. This is true for you—our God can get your dad out of prison. This is an easy thing for Jesus. I am asking, trusting, and believing with you that God will do this soon.

"But . . . " the three Hebrew young men go on (Daniel 3:18), ". . . even if he does not, . . . we will not serve your gods . . . "(NIV) God delivers His children usually in one of three ways:

a) Escape—He gets us out of difficult situations (like the apostles in Acts 5:19 and Peter in Acts 12:10 being miraculously rescued from prison).

b) Endurance—God helps us to persevere through difficult periods of prison and suffering (like Joseph in prison for many years; Jeremiah in the bottom of the well; Paul spending several years in prison in Rome).

c) Eternity—God takes us home to heaven where we are forever delivered from all evil—harm, pain, sadness, sickness, and loss.

We don't always get to choose how God delivers us (and of course it is natural to want "Escape") but we do have this confidence: God always delivers! God always wins in the end! Our God will deliver us.

5) The suffering your family is experiencing is normal.

What you as a family are experiencing (your dad, your mom, you as children) is the normal Christian life for all who radically follow Jesus. You are not special (either in the bad way, being picked on, or in the good way, being better than anyone else). The Bible says in Philippians 1:29, "For it has been granted (given) to you on behalf of Christ, not only to believe in Him, but also to suffer for Him." (NIV) And in 2 Timothy 3:12, ". . . everyone who desires to live a godly life in Christ Jesus will be persecuted." (NIV)

All through history, across every nation, men and women, moms and dads, boys and girls have suffered and are suffering for Jesus. You are not alone, and some have it much worse than you, much worse than your father. In the Holy Spirit you are connected in an intimate way to a vast army of Jesus followers who have been given the privilege of suffering for Jesus. Welcome to the family! The family who loves Jesus so much it is an honor to suffer for His sake!

When the apostles were imprisoned and beaten they were ". . . rejoicing that they were counted worthy to suffer . . ." (Acts 5:41) and they responded by continuing publicly and privately to teach and preach that Jesus is the Christ (Acts 5:42). Suffering made them bolder, they did not cease proclaiming Jesus everywhere. Jesus evidently looks at your family, loves you deeply, trusts you fully, so much that He says, "Look at them! They are worthy to suffer for my name. I trust them to continue to teach and preach about me!" Oh, how much the Heavenly Father loves and trusts you!

6) It is the devil you should be angry at, not the people who put your dad in prison.

In Luke 23:34 when Jesus is being crucified, he says: ". . . Father, forgive them, for they know not what they do. . . ." Really, the people who put your dad in prison (and the people group* and country they represent) are not angry at him, they are angry at Jesus—even if they don't know it. All false religions deny that Jesus is God, and the devil (often without the people realizing it) stirs them up to attack anyone who believes that Jesus is God and super exalts Him as the only way of salvation.

When people do hurtful things to us, it is important to recognize that the source of their anger is fear—the fear of the devil because he knows Jesus is winning and he hates Jesus. When we understand this, it helps us to direct our anger at the devil and not at the precious people we live among. Always remember the people you live among are precious to Jesus. They are victims of the devil's lies. We forgive them because they don't really know what they are doing, they don't realize they are actually fighting against the spirit of

Jesus in us—this is a fight they cannot win. We love them because even though pain comes through their hands, we realize that the source of their evil actions is the devil.

7) Your father wants you to go on living and in fact to have joy!

In John 19:26–27 when Jesus was in great trouble in the cross, He was most concerned about His friends and family. Your father (whether he is taken from you for a short time or long) wants you to live well and to love life. Sometimes we feel guilty about laughing or doing normal life and fun things when our father is in prison. We can feel guilty about laughing, visiting friends, playing football, and moving on in life in a normal way—when inside we know our father is gone and life is not normal.

What your father wants is for you to live free and he would be most pleased if you continue to embrace life and find joy despite your sorrow. There are times to cry and miss him and grieve, but joy and sorrow are not opposites. They can go together. You can carry the sorrow of missing your father and the joy of living and laughing in life—and this is not hypocritical.

> There are times to cry and miss him and grieve, but joy and sorrow are not opposites.

Laughter and tears are brothers. They are intended to live together. Perfect, sinless, eternal Jesus both laughed and cried.

When we laugh, when we continue the normal activities of life despite living in abnormal conditions, when we laugh along with our sorrow we are sending two messages:

1. We are telling God that as much as we love our earthly father, we love our heavenly Father even more and we trust Him. This delights Him. When we praise Jesus despite our troubles, when it costs us to praise Him and trust Him (when we bring ". . . sacrifices with shouts of joy . . ." Psalm 27:6) we please our heavenly Father incredibly.

2. *We communicate to the devil that he is a loser, that he never can win. Jesus will win; the devil will lose. We are celebrating the end result even while we are in the middle of the struggle with much pain. You will most honor your heavenly and earthly fathers by living well and laughing with joy—along with your sorrow.*

Conclusion:

Jesus loves you so much, and your father loves you so much. In his prison, he is not thinking about his ministry or even his friends or the people he has brought to Jesus. Do you know who your dad spends most of his time thinking about? You! Your father is praying for you, and remembering all the good times you had together, and laughing at all the funny things you did when you were small, and wondering how you are doing in school, and hoping you remembered to brush your teeth this morning. He misses his wife and his children more than anything.

Your father wants you to know again that you are more important to him than any other human or any work that he has done. He loves you, loves you, loves you. You are his pride and joy. He may not be able to see you or hug you or even speak with you, but his spirit sends a constant message. Your father says "I love you, I love you, I love you. You are my beloved child. In you I am well pleased."

So Ezekiel and Lea, these are challenging days, but you will make it. You will make it because God is good and He loves you, because your father and mother love you, because your uncles and aunts and friends around the world love you and are praying for you.

Your father wants you to live and love and laugh. You will best please him by mixing your joy into your sorrow, carrying them both, and trusting Jesus to help you. Keep doing the normal things of life (knowing this is what your father would want, doing them even for him) and in the quiet times when you most miss him and feel his absence, it is OK to cry. Perhaps in those times, write him a letter in your journal, tell him the things you cannot tell anyone else. Tell him the simple things; tell him the serious things. Pray for him (and your mom), and then rest in the knowledge that your father loves you very, very much and that he loves Jesus so much that this suffering of separation (that you all share) is worth it because Jesus is worth it.

We are so very proud of you.
We love you so very much.

18

EZEKIEL'S STORY

My name is Ezekiel. When my dad was in prison, I was thirteen years old. During this time I had many thoughts and feelings. This period of my life helped me come closer to God. My dad faced this time with courage. I am proud of my dad.

One afternoon when my dad came home from his course to become a certified English teacher, he asked me if I wanted to join him in the English center upstairs. I gladly went. We arrived at the center. There were men there that immediately asked my dad to talk with him in a separate room. I recognized them as security.

After about ten minutes Dad came out with a look on his face that showed me that something was happening. He ordered me to run down the stairs, get my small laptop, get my phone, and bring it to him. I ran down. I quickly told my mom what Dad had said while I got the phone and computer. I left the house again.

Dad was already waiting at the door with the other men. I gave him the two things. Dad briefly said goodbye to our family and left. A minute after he left I realized that my dad might not know the password for my phone. I ran out of the house and followed the men. I told him the code in our mother tongue. Then he left. This was the last time I saw him for eighteen days.

I went back home. I was confused. I was slightly angry and mad at those men that ordered my dad to leave. I was scared. I did not know what would happen now. We ate dinner and went to bed not knowing what would happen next.

The next day was a school day. We went to school as usual. At school my thoughts always drifted back to the things that had happened the day before. I asked myself many times, "What will happen next?" The next five days were like this one.

On day six, one of my dad's friends, Jack, sent my mom an email that contained a letter for my sister and me. He said: "Yesterday I was thinking about what I would want someone to tell my boys if I were in prison. Here is what I would want them to know." That evening my mom read the letter to us. This letter really encouraged me. It reassured me that God was totally in control. He loved me. He loved my dad, and He loved my family. I got to know that our family was glorifying God by suffering for him. I was reassured that my dad would be delivered someday either by an escape, through endurance, or in eternity. We were not the only ones that suffer for Christ. A lot of people were in a situation far worse than ours. This letter helped me to stop my anger against the security. I tried to love them, bless them, and pray for them. I did not feel bad any more when I was really enjoying something. I got to know that my dad wanted me to be happy and enjoy myself. This letter really helped me to be able to go through the next fifty-one days without my dad.

Before the letter, it was quite hard for me to respect my mom and to be kind to my sister. The next few days were easier for me. We went to school as usual. Sometimes we went to our friends' houses because mom was driving around to find out about dad. My sister and I really appreciated those visits. As my mom already mentioned, there was a young man that lived in our flat. I called him Luemel. He played and spent a lot of time with Lea and me. We enjoyed several ice creams with Luemel. My neighbor friend often came to play with me. He knew nothing about the situation. We shared a few chickens. We tried to continue to live out our daily life.

My mom found out how we could drop off food and clothes for Dad. She also found out that the law said that after about fifteen days one could request to see a prisoner. We asked to see Dad. A few days later a phone call came, we were told that our request had been accepted. I was so excited.

We went to visit him on day eighteen. We arrived at the prison. The security guards brought us into a small room with a couch and a few armchairs. Then they gave orders to bring Dad. The door was left slightly open. After a while we heard voices and footsteps. Dad! We saw him before he saw us. He was quite pale, had longer hair than usual, and had not shaved. That shocked me a bit. He was looking at the guards a bit confused. The look was like: "Oh, no, will they question me again?" When he stepped into the room his face lit up. He was not expecting us at all. He was so happy and immediately sat down between my sister and me. He began to rub our bellies. He told us over and over again that he loved us. He said that God was speaking to him a lot, and that God was in control. He said that he was treated well. This really helped me to go through the hard time. Dad also told us to go to a nice hotel during our upcoming school break. We told him that we could only visit him every twenty days. Then we said our goodbyes and left the prison.

The next few days were again mostly normal school days. My mom tried to keep our lives as normal as possible. For example, we kept the same meal times. We could not entirely continue with our normal life, mainly because Dad was not with us. Every member plays a huge role in the family. People especially notice what role others play when they are not around. This was a situation like that. We had packed all we needed to take with us if suddenly the security said that we had to leave. This was also another factor that made living a normal life a bit harder, but it really helped remove the concern of not having enough time to pack everything if we suddenly had to leave.

After about fifteen days, Mom made another request to see Dad. The security confirmed and said we could go see him on day thirty-one of his imprisonment. I was happy, but I was not sure if I really wanted to go see him. After the first visit, I missed him more than before. Seeing him made me miss him very much.

My mom felt that God had told her that our time in this country was finished for the moment. She talked about this with some of my dad's close friends. They felt the same way. We were planning to tell him that on our visit. Last time the security guards let my sister and me speak our mother tongue with Dad. Mom prepared my sister and me to tell my dad that we thought that our time in the country was coming to an end. She told us what to say to Dad if we were able to speak in our mother tongue again. She also said that we could sing a song to Dad in our mother tongue, if we were not able to talk to him. We would have made up a song on the spot containing the things my mom wanted to tell him.

We got ready to see him. I was very happy. So we went to the prison. Again we waited in the room we were in last visit. This time Dad was expecting us. He came in and greeted the security and us quickly. He sat down between my sister and me. Unlike last time, this time he sat upright and started to talk to us straight away. He said something like this in our mother tongue: "OK, Ezekiel and Lea, now I will talk to you, and Mom has to listen very carefully. I will tell Mom what I want her to do. I want that you . . ." Dad was looking at us and pretending to talk to us, but actually he shared his thoughts with Mom. He talked like a news reporter, because he stated one thought after the other without even letting Lea and me say our opinion. We did nod, though, and said, "Yes" so that it would look like we were actually the ones to whom Dad was talking.

After about five minutes, Dad relaxed from his upright sitting position and leaned back on the sofa with us. He started telling us how much he loved us and how God spoke to him. Again he rubbed our bellies. I told Dad that we also felt that it might be good to try to leave the country. I thought it might be good that Dad would know too. When I told him that, he was very happy. The rest of the visit we just enjoyed spending time with Dad.

We left the prison happy, because we were able to see Dad. We also left sad, because we all really missed Dad. I was also sad because now I knew that we would leave the country soon.

The next few days we started making piles from our stuff. We tagged the piles as "to be sold," "to be given as a gift," or "to be given to . . ." If we suddenly had to leave, we wanted to spend more time in our goodbyes than in packing. We got ready to leave.

The time came for another visit. This time there was nothing important to tell Dad except, "We love and miss you." I was looking forward to this visit. Like before, I knew that I would miss Dad more after the visit, but seeing Dad was just what I wanted. Again we went to the prison and then waited in the same room as the two other times. Again I sat next to Dad during the visit. One thing I remember about the visit is that I had this good pride. I was very proud of my dad. I knew God spoke to him a lot during this time. I was just proud. This was on the fiftieth day of my dad's time with security.

The next six days were like the ones before the visit. I missed Dad so much. The fifty-seventh day of my dad's imprisonment was another school day. My sister's class left for a three-day (two nights) field trip in the desert. On that same day, I had a soccer game against another school. My mom's friends came to watch me play and then to take me home. Our school won that game five to three. After the game, my mom's friend explained to me that Mom was at the police office, and Dad was there too. They brought me home. Mom arrived shortly after and explained to me that Dad was OK, but was now in a police station. We would have to bring him stuff he could sleep on.

We arrived at the station. There were people walking around everywhere. We were able to give him the sleeping stuff. We also gave him a bag with a phone in it. The guard saw the phone and did not want to let it through. We also gave him an exercise mat. My dad told the officer that he could have the mat if he would give him the phone. The guy agreed. I thought that my dad was funny. Then Dad even asked me if I would like to sleep a night with him in the prison. I thought it might be nice, but I had school the next day. And even if I had wanted to stay in the prison, the guard would not have allowed it. I still remember this very well. I was glad that I was able to see Dad.

The next day was again a school day. I went to school and came back home. Luemel was waiting for me there. He said that Dad would leave the country that night. I was very happy. Mom came back and explained that we would leave the next day, and not with Dad, because Lea was still in the desert. I had a lot of homework over the weekend. I told Mom that I would not have to do it because the next day would be the last day in my beloved country! Again I went with Mom to the police station because we had to help Dad with something.

That night became a very crazy, but fun night. I came home at about nine o'clock. I went on the computer and wrote an email to all my classmates saying that I would be leaving the next day. I was amazed at how many people checked email and replied at this hour. After this I went to my neighbor, my best local friend. I gave him some of the things we both had played with during the time we had spent together. He said that there was a football final between the two main rivals of the country. We watched that game together. I really enjoyed it. It was a good way of saying goodbye to my friend. At eleven we went back to my house. We talked for a while. When he left I was really sad. Mom and I went to tell someone that we were leaving. When we came back, a guy took a lot of our spices. He left at twelve o'clock, midnight! After that we left to go to the airport to bring Dad his luggage. We arrived at the airport at one in the morning. Around one thirty the security brought my dad to the airport. We said our goodbyes and left. Finally, I went to bed at three in the morning.

After three hours I woke up to go to school. That day we had an art field trip planned to the National Museum. We left at the beginning of the school day. The friend I was closest with organized a poster with everyone's name on it. That was really nice. We went back to school. Mom picked Lea and me up, and we went home. We packed up the last things. People came to visit us and say their goodbyes. This was my last day.

Lea and I went to sleep a bit early because we would have to wake up at one in the morning to go to the airport. We went to the airport. We boarded the plane. I remember looking out of the window until I could see no light of the city anymore. I knew that we could not return to this country for a while. We went to a nearby country and enjoyed the trees, but I personally prefer the hot and dry desert of my country. The desert had been my home for my whole life.

I felt both very happy and very sad when we left. I was very sad because I had to leave all my friends. Goodbyes are very hard. I had to leave the desert. The hardest thing was to leave the place I call home. I know, though, that this is God's plan. The best and safest place a human can be is where God wants him to be. I gladly accept God's plan for our family. So I said my goodbyes. Who knows if God will call you or me to that country one day?

My happiness was that we were going to be reunited again as a family. These two months I really got to understand the important role each family member plays in a family. When my sister would be gone for a sleepover at a friend's house, there was something missing, but it was soon restored. When my dad or mom went on a trip there was also something missing, but I knew it would be restored soon. We were always able to connect on Skype. I guess my family feels the same way if I am not in the house. With these situations something is missing, and one knows that everything will be the way it was very quickly. With Dad in prison there

> The best and safest place a human can be is where God wants him to be.

was something missing in the family, and I did not know when this would be restored. Not being able to talk to Dad made it worse. So I am glad that the thing missing was restored. We played a lot with Dad during our vacation after he was released, and we still do today.

Like many times in the Christian history, when Christians are persecuted in any way, their faith grows a lot. It was like this for our whole family. This situation helped my trust in God grow so much. During the situation, I knew God was in control. I got to know God better in this situation.

A thing that also really helped me was that there was nothing wrong between Dad and me when he left. That would have been horrible if I would not have been sure that everything was good between us. Another thing that helped me go through this time is that I read a series called "Trailblazers." This series tells about missionaries of old times like Adoniram Judson, Hudson Taylor, Jim Elliot, Amy Carmichael, and many others. I still read these today. These books helped because they showed how the missionaries had to suffer for Christ. Even most of the apostles died for Christ. Suffering for Christ is part of being a follower of Jesus. Two months of suffering for Christ is a small thing compared to spending eternity with Him. It was totally worth it.

Mom was another huge help to me during this time. She always encouraged me. She helped us not to be mad at security, but to love them and forgive them. She helped us say goodbye to the country. In the last few days, she helped us see our friends and go to our favorite places in the country. I was very proud of my mom. She took control of our family.

When I grow up I want to be like my dad. I am proud of him. I thank God that we were able to honor him by suffering for God. The letter of my dad's friend really helped me go through this time. It also confirmed what the most important thing is in a situation like this and any time in life. It is "to know that God is in control and He loves you so much."

19

LEA'S STORY

My name is Lea. I was almost eleven years old when all of this happened. When my dad was in prison for such a long time, more than ever before I realized how thoughts and emotions wanted to rule my head and heart. Every day there were a lot of things happening; some were easy to face and others were hard. To overcome and stay strong was a decision of my heart and not of my feelings. One thing that really helped me is that my mom encouraged me to start writing a kind of a diary for my dad. I started on the fourteenth day of his imprisonment. I started to write him daily letters. At that time, we had not seen him since the day he was taken. I wrote:

October 15, 2012
Dear Dad,
How are you? I am fine. What does the prison look like? Do you share your room with our teammate who is also arrested? Do you have enough food and water? Did they give or lend you a Bible? Do they treat you well? How long can you sleep? Where do you sleep?
Sincerely,
Your daughter, Lea

October 17, 2012

Dear Dad,

I pray for you a lot. I know that God is with you. I also know that God always does the best for us. I also know that God wants to teach us something. God is trying us. God always makes us able to stand up while trying us and never makes it too big. That is why I pray for you so much.

Sincerely,
Your daughter, Lea

October 19, 2012

Dear Dad,

I am very sad, because I miss you so much. Mom told me that it is normal that we are sad and sometimes worry. Uncle Jack told me that I should be happy that Jesus trusts you to go to prison! I believed him and asked Mom if she could pray for me. After she prayed for me, I felt so much better.

Sincerely,
Your daughter, Lea

October 21, 2012

Dear Dad,

Do you know the significance of the symbol of a dove? It means peace. I believe that we should go through this situation peacefully. God always wants to give us his peace which is different compared to human peace. This is why I think that we should always reach out for the peace of God.

Sincerely,
Your daughter, Lea

October 26, 2012
Dear Dad,

Good morning! How are you? I am fine. In the night, I woke up. Then I saw a scary face down at Mom's feet. My first idea was to pray. I prayed and then the scary face was gone. (I didn't see it anymore.) That made me really happy. Then, I worshiped and praised God.

Sincerely,
Your daughter, Lea

October 27, 2012
Dear Dad,

I picture you like a strong and mighty lion. You are like the lion who is the king of all the animals. You are an absolutely reliable ruler and leader of our family. You stand up in easy and hard situations for our family. You are also incredibly brave. You are a wonderful dad for all of us. You read the Bible so often and you always pray for us. You practice everything that is written in Galatians 5:22. I love and miss you in an indescribable way.

Sincerely,
Your daughter, Lea

November 5, 2012
Dear Dad,

Good morning! How are you? I am fine. Do you remember that I often have dreams? I dreamed last night that our arrested team member was again with his family. After that I dreamed that you, too, were again with us. After that dream, I understood that we have to leave the country we are living in. I also saw that our teammate met his family before you were with us. I do not know when this dream will be fulfilled, but I know it is going to happen sooner or later.

Sincerely,
Your daughter, Lea

Having Luemel, "my mother's younger brother," living with us was also a huge help. He played with us, helped with my computer homework, drove us to events, and sometimes picked us up from school. We laughed a lot together even in the midst of the pressure. Also we shared many mealtimes together. He was also a huge help as he seemed to understand how much we missed our dad. When I cried, he tried, and sometimes even succeeded, to comfort me.

Every Friday, after the international church service, one of my two favorite teachers took time with me, and we prayed! With this teacher I was allowed to share anything and everything.

Sharing openly with my friend, Lily, was a big help too. Although we were not in the same classroom, we were riding the same school bus. There, I had a chance to talk to her. Since their family also started to experience some pressure from the secret police, I could give her encouragement and advice at the same time. The last time Lily came for a sleepover (we didn't know it was going to be the last time) we had a real party; we will always remember and never forget. I wrote in my diary:

> *November 25, 2013*
> *Dear Dad,*
>
> *Good morning! How are you today? I am 100 percent fine, but also I feel a little bit tired. Yesterday, Lily came to us for a sleepover. We ate waffles with strawberry sauce, cream, and icing sugar. We played a special game and that is how it went: Lily had two "Chinese Jump Ropes" and cards that told us how we should jump over the ropes. It was very funny, and I really enjoyed it. You should have seen me do it because I wasn't that good at it and looked really funny!*
>
> > *Sincerely,*
> > *Your daughter, Lea*

On day fifty-seven of my dad's imprisonment, the sixth grade had a camping trip to the pyramids and the "mountains," basically a huge pile of gigantic rocks. The day before (actually my last diary entry when Dad was away), I wrote:

November 26, 2012
Dear Dad,

How are you? I am fine. I am very happy and nervous, because tomorrow I am going on ODE, Outdoor Education. ODE is when one's whole grade is going on a camping trip. Our camping trip lasts two nights and three days. The first night we have to be in bed at 9:30 p.m., and the second night we have to be in bed at 9:45 p.m., but both nights we can also go earlier. Both mornings we have to wake up at 6:00 a.m.

Sincerely,
Your daughter, Lea

On the second day while we were climbing the "mountains" the first time, my ODE teacher had a call from our principal. The call was about a child having to leave. Right away I knew it was me. When he was done talking on the phone, I went and asked him to make 100 percent sure it really was me, and I wanted to know what he had heard. He just said that my mom would phone me later. I was almost sure that it meant I had to leave. Later, when Mom phoned me, she told me that we had to leave and that Dad had to fly out that night, but she and Ezekiel would wait for me, and we would fly out the night after my return. I heard my dad's voice, too, which I hadn't heard for a long time. (He had been moved from prison to the police station). Hearing their voices, especially Dad's, encouraged me a lot. I felt 100 percent glad to know that I was going to see my dad very soon, but at the same time, I was very sad to leave one of my most home-like countries. I told Lily what Mom and Dad had told me, and we cried together until we couldn't any more. While crying, Lily called all the curious sixth grade girls together and said that I had to leave for good because of some visa problems. One of the boys threw goat poop at us, but we didn't care at all. None of the boys knew why all the girls were crying. All the teachers allowed Lily and me to sleep in the same tent, even though we originally had other tent mates. The boys wanted to encourage the girls, even though they didn't know what had happened, so they said, "Let's play Capture the Flag!" Even though it was a lot of fun trying, we didn't actually win. The last breakfast I had was a local bean dish, eggs, and bread. The local dish is beans, sesame oil, and a type of spice. Even though I had never liked it, I made up my mind I should eat it because it was probably the last time I could eat it, so I ate. I can't believe it actually tasted much better than the best French fries!

After that most wonderful breakfast, we drove from the desert back to school in town. I was picked up by Mom and our wonderful friend who supported Mom throughout that whole day. Again, Mom blessed us with a special lunch by picking up a pizza topped with eggplant slices and parmesan cheese from our favorite pizza place. That afternoon and evening were filled with packing, goodbyes with tears, and flying out to a nearby country where my dad had travelled the night before.

At seven a.m. the next day, we arrived in the land of elephants and lions. We were all super tired but almost couldn't wait to go through customs to meet Dad and be together again with him and reunited as a family. When we finally were able to go out, we were welcomed by my dad and Uncle Jack, the guy who wrote us that most helpful letter when Dad was in prison. Dad had brought gifts with him for all three of us. He gave my mom a beautiful bouquet of red roses, my brother two lollipops, and me a charming red rose and two lollipops! Finally my dream came to its fulfillment: we had to leave our beloved country of ministry where we felt at home, but were reunited as a family again!

PART 2

20

AN EXHORTATION
FROM GOD

Now that you know a lot of my story, you have discovered that God
has given me a passion for church planting among unreached tribes
and untouched cities and villages. I consider this calling a great
privilege and an honor. Nothing in this world excites me more than being
part of expanding God's kingdom.

As you learned while reading about my experience in prison, God revealed
many things to me. Much of what He revealed to me was related to planting
churches* among unreached peoples. He confirmed things that I had known
from my past experiences, and He showed me some new things as well. He
shared part of His heart with me, but I knew at the time that this was not
just for me. These encouragements and exhortations are for the people who
have wondered if God might be calling them to cross a culture and bring the
gospel to those who have never heard. They are for the new church planter
who is eager to learn more about church planting. And they are for the
church planter who wants to evaluate his work and to improve. I pray this
next section brings you vision and hope while equipping you practically for
the greatest and most wonderful commission from our Lord Jesus: to go and
make disciples of all nations.

In my sixteen years of church planting among unreached peoples (mainly
Muslim peoples), I have seen many different strategies come and go. I have seen
strategies blessed by God when I thought they never should have worked, and
I have seen the best strategies, which were proven elsewhere, not bear any fruit

in a different place. Sometimes people who have seen much fruit in one place use the same "fruitful" strategy in a different place and see little or no fruit.

We are eager for upgrading and want to use the best strategies the Holy Spirit reveals for church planting in our time. Jesus himself used so many different ways of preaching, healing, approaching people, and sharing the gospel. Strategies change as the Lord reveals different ways of reaching out to communities. However, the twelve concepts in the following section of this book contain principles that don't change. These principles are related more to the character of a church planter rather than to a certain strategy related to a people group or culture. These principles should not change. The church planter should grow in these areas as well as in his daily walk with God.

Church planting is a task that demands a long-term commitment, especially when we talk about reaching out to those who have never heard the gospel. In my relatively short time as a church planter, I have seen many people "burn out." I believe that these principles will help church planters to keep the first things first so that they can last and at the appointed time, see the fruit that the Lord will give them through their faithful labor among unreached peoples.

TWELVE PRINCIPLES FOR CHURCH PLANTING

1 Praise	5 Passion and Purpose	9 Proximate belivers
2 Purification	6 Power	10 Presence in a community
3 Prayer	7 Perseverance	11 Partners
4 Proclamation	8 Persecution	12 Pitfalls

A note to the reader who is not a cross-cultural church planter ...

In this section, I talk mainly about church planters because that is my area of expertise and where the majority of my life experience lies. However, these principles and truths apply to anyone with a desire to see and be part of the advancement of God's kingdom. Make no mistake, pastors, employees, business owners, homemakers, mothers, children, students, and grandparents ... these truths are for you too. In fact, I wrote chapter 27 with you specifically in mind.

21

PRAISE

Often when we use the phrase "praise and worship," we think of singing a few songs at the beginning of a church service. When I talk about praise and worship, I am referring to our whole demeanor and attitude toward Him. Every thought and action is an offering of worship to our God.

A church planter often has so many things to do in his daily schedule that the worship of our God is neglected or even totally abandoned. Mission and strategy and the many other good things that we do on earth will be finished and cease to exist in heaven, but worship and praise will continue forever. Our God is a God who wants to be praised and worshiped—He is glorified and honored when His children worship Him. We must spend time daily worshiping the Lord and giving Him all the

> Mission and strategy will be finished and cease to exist in heaven, but worship and praise will continue forever.

praise and honor He is worthy to receive. Worship does many things in the heart of a church planter that are crucial for his daily work.

1. Worship puts God in His rightful position.

When we worship the Lord, we turn our faces and our thoughts away from ourselves towards our wise, majestic, and powerful Father in heaven. We recognize that He is Lord; He has been Lord, and He will ever be Lord over all.

While I spent time with the Lord on a regular basis before I was imprisoned, it was not enough. I got so busy with ministry that my time with the Lord lost its quality and some of its quantity. In my case, the Lord intervened by taking me out of the daily work to spend time with Him alone when I was put in prison. For the apostles, we see in Acts 6:4 that the Holy Spirit reminded them to change their focus and spend more time in prayer and in the Word. When I read the psalms aloud every day, I felt the Lord's pleasure in hearing worship come out of the mouth of one of his followers.

2. Worship invites God to fight our battles.
God inhabits the praises of His people, and His presence brings victory over the darkness of the enemy. The battle of Jericho was won with worship.

Joshua 6:20 *"So the people shouted, and the trumpets were blown. As soon as the people heard the sound of the trumpet, the people shouted a great shout, and the wall fell down flat, so that the people went up into the city, every man straight before him, and they captured the city."*

Paul and Silas were freed from prison when they worshiped.

Acts 16:25–26 *"About midnight Paul and Silas were praying and singing hymns to God, and the prisoners were listening to them, and suddenly there was a great earthquake, so that the foundations of the prison were shaken. And immediately all the doors were opened, and everyone's bonds were unfastened."*

3. Worship renews the strength of a worker.
As church planters, we must stay close to Jesus because we can do nothing out of our own wisdom and strength. It is only what we do out of the deep relationship with our Lord that lasts for eternity. So many people start church planting full of zeal and commitment. However, many church planters do not last long because they burn out or lose vision for the work. One of the primary reasons for this is that their spiritual batteries are chronically low or empty. Jesus called his disciples to be with Him first and then to go and share the good news.

Mark 3:14 *"And he appointed twelve, that they might be with him, and that he might send them out to preach."*

John 15:4 *"Abide in me, and I in you. As the branch cannot bear fruit by itself, unless it abides in the vine, neither can you, unless you abide in me."*

When the church planting work goes badly (key believers fall into sin; nobody wants to hear the name of Jesus; the team has problems; or financial support decreases), drawing near to Jesus in worship expresses our deep need for Him and renews our strength.

If we do not go to the Fountain and Source to be filled up, we will have nothing of eternal value to offer the people around us.

Jesus affirmed Mary in Luke 10 for sitting at His feet. We must do likewise and sit at the feet of Jesus often if we want to have the strength to continue the work. If we do not go to the Fountain and Source to be filled up, we will have nothing of eternal value to offer the people around us.

CHALLENGE

Choose at least one of the following.
For the next 40 days:

- Tithe your time. Give 2.4 hours/day to the Lord through worship, prayer, and reading his word.
- Spend a 5-hour chunk of time every week with the Lord in prayer and worship. Schedule it on your calendar as you would schedule any other appointment in your life.

Start date: _____

End date: _____

Name of the person who can support you as you complete this challenge:

_____

22

PURIFICATION

Jeremiah 17:10 "*I the LORD search the heart and test the mind, to give every man according to his ways, according to the fruit of his deeds.*"

Romans 2:16 "*On that day when, according to my gospel, God judges the secrets of men by Christ Jesus.*"

1 Corinthians 4:4–5 "*For I am not aware of anything against myself, but I am not thereby acquitted. It is the Lord who judges me. Therefore do not pronounce judgment before the time, before the Lord comes, who will bring to light the things now hidden in darkness and will disclose the purposes of the heart. Then each one will receive his commendation from God.*"

We live in a fallen world and are surrounded by spiritual forces that influence us. We must guard our hearts, especially from hidden sins like pride, jealousy, bitterness, lust, unforgiveness, and gossip. If Satan overcomes our hearts with his strategies, he knows that we will lose our effectiveness in advancing the kingdom.

> Do not let the sun go down while keeping something in your heart against anyone.

How can we purify our hearts so that we can resist the devil's schemes?

1. Do not sleep until your heart is cleansed by the blood of Jesus.
Do not let the sun go down while keeping something in your heart against anyone. Many church planters are attacked in this area. It seems that we have the least difficulty forgiving the people we are trying to reach with the gospel because we expect them to be difficult and to reject the gospel and us. Our

close relationships with our spouses or teammates, on the other hand, can often be the most difficult and hurtful. I have seen unforgiveness send workers back to their home countries and break up teams and even marriages.

2. Let the Holy Spirit search your heart and mind.

We must regularly give the Holy Spirit a chance to reveal the sin in our hearts. When I was in prison, the Lord showed me sin in my heart like pride and jealousy of which I was not at all aware. Whether we are aware or not, Jesus knows it all. We need to let God search our hearts over and over again, and we need to seek the holiness of Jesus in our lives. What a shame it would be to stand before the Lord only to realize that He could have delivered me and washed me clean from the sin I carried for such a long time if I had only let Him reveal it to me. Remind yourself daily that Jesus knows it all. This might help you from keeping anything in your heart hidden.

> Remind yourself daily that Jesus knows it all. This might help you from keeping anything in your heart hidden.

We must be aware of our weaknesses and pray regularly for God's grace in those areas. Be honest with yourself and do not put yourself into situations where you know that the devil could easily attack you in your areas of weakness.

Do you know what your weaknesses are? It is good to be aware of them so that you can pray about them and have other people pray with you in those areas.

3. Take communion together.

According to 1 Corinthians 11:23–34, it is good to take the Lord's Supper regularly. Take note especially of verses 28 and 29 regarding the manner in which we should take it:

"Let a person examine himself, then, and so eat of the bread and drink of the cup. For anyone who eats and drinks without discerning the body eats and drinks judgment on himself."

Celebrating the Lord's Supper together as a church planting team helps to keep the relationships within the team holy and purified while causing us to slow down enough to examine our hearts before the Lord and if needed, confess and repent.

4. Have an accountability partner of the same sex with whom you can share your life.

Ask each other the tough questions, and pray for each other in the areas of each other's weaknesses.

The following are some sample questions that might be helpful. Some of these questions are very private and personal, but these are precisely the areas where the enemy will try to bring you down. You do not have to share this with many people, just with one or two people whom you trust, who want God's best for you and who will pray with you in these areas.

Have him or her ask these or similar questions on a regular basis:
- Have your words in the past week testified to the glory of Jesus Christ?
- Did you pray every day of the week?
- Did you tell the truth at all times and in all circumstances?
- Did you have impure thoughts about a woman who is not your wife or a man who is not your husband?
- Did you act wrongly against your neighbor, either in actions or in words? Did you speak poorly of him behind his back or to his face? Did you spread bad rumors?
- Do you lack peace in your heart related to a person or a fact?
- Are you in danger of getting prideful in any area of your life?
- Did you handle your money well or did you waste it on useless things? Did you tithe?
- Have you fulfilled the mandate of your calling?
- Personal question :

———————————————————

By adding a personal question, you reveal to your partner an area of weakness where you want him to keep you accountable. This will help you to resist the devil and his schemes against you and protect the ministry the Lord has entrusted to you.

It is common for issues like money, sex, and pride to be the most challenging areas of temptation for men, especially church planters. The story of the rise and fall of a young church planter named Thomas illustrates the sobriety with which we should treat the issue of personal holiness. This individual accepted the Lord when he was a young man and was used by God to plant house churches* in his own country among Muslims. Thomas moved to another country in West Africa and again was one of the most successful church planters in that area. He got married and was sent by a local church to another North African country where he was very respected by the missions community. But at some point, the devil gained a foothold in his heart in the area of pride. He felt that his wife was dishonoring him, but he did not share this with anybody. Thomas started stealing money from a cash box, and later he started visiting prostitutes at night. No one knew about any of these things because he would tell people that he was visiting friends and sharing Jesus with them. Thomas started beating his wife, but she was too ashamed to tell anyone. Later on he tried to kill his wife by driving the car into a tree on the side where she sat. At the time, it just looked like an accident, so no one thought anything of it. A year later Thomas stabbed his wife with a knife. Eventually, he confessed and told us the whole story.

This is a horrible story and an extreme situation, but unfortunately it is true. Let us not forget the story of King David's adultery and murder as he opened the door to the devil through lust in his heart. The devil is a roaring lion and he seeks to destroy whomever he can, especially those who work among the unreached.

CHALLENGE

Choose at least one of the following.

- If you do not already have an accountability partner, ask God to provide you with someone and then be silent and wait for the answer. Write the name of the person or people.

If you didn't hear anything or think of anyone, persistently ask God to provide someone until He does. If you live in a place where you are isolated, consider a regular Skype appointment with someone.

- Write out a commitment to God that you will not let the sun go down without asking Him if there is any unforgiveness in your heart and then extending that forgiveness.

_____

_____

- If you do not do so already, talk with your team leader or colleagues about taking the Lord's Supper regularly with your team.
- Ask the Lord to show you any unconfessed sin in your life and write it down along with the name of a person to whom you can confess.

_____

_____

_____

- Ask the Lord, your spouse, or a good friend, and yourself what your areas of weakness are. Write them down and then list one or two ways to avoid situations which give the devil space to attack you in those areas.

_____

_____

_____

23

PRAYER

1. Pray on your own.

Nothing can replace the personal prayer of a church planter. It is important to make sure that we plan regular times where we can pray and seek the Lord. While presenting our requests to God is important, prayer is so much more than that. Spend time listening to learn what the Father is doing and to know the works that the Lord has prepared for you to do. Let God remind you of His vision for your life and empower you to be the person He made you to be and to do the things that He wants you to do. "Prayer does not fit us for the greater work; prayer is the greater work."[1]

> "Prayer does not fit us for the greater work; prayer is the greater work."

2. Pray with other believers.

Church planters on the same team or in the same city or region should regularly take time to come together and pray for the activities of their church planting efforts. Praying with others is often a great encouragement, and it keeps the church planter focused on the task at hand. It is important when you come together as a group that you also spend time listening to what the Lord has to say about specific situations.

---

1   Oswald Chambers, *My Utmost for His Highest* (Grand Rapids, Michigan: Discovery House Publishers, 1963).

The danger of a group prayer meeting is that people end up talking and listening more to each other than to God. To guard against this, have an agenda for your allotted time of prayer. For example, you could use an hour of prayer like this: twenty minutes of worship and listening to the Lord, twenty minutes of sharing about the general church planting situation, and then twenty minutes of guided intercession for the mentioned topics. In one of the teams I led, we started our workday every day by praying for an hour. Prayer is part of our work! Whether it is business, NGO work, or any other job we do as church planters, we need to make prayer our priority and make time to do it.

3. Recruit a prayer and fasting team for you and the people group.

One hundred years ago, cross-cultural workers had one option for communication with their friends and family: snail mail. When we started church planting sixteen years ago, our access to email was spotty, unreliable, expensive, and extremely slow during the best times. Praise the Lord for modern technology. Today, we can inform supporters all over the world of prayer needs in a matter of minutes.

4. Pray with the people you want to reach.

When we pray with people who are not yet believers in Jesus, we show them that we trust the Lord to answer our prayers. This is a very powerful tool to use with Muslims, but can be used with anyone. The Bible tells us many times that we should bless people, and when we pray for people's needs, we follow these commands:

Luke 6:28 *"Bless those who curse you, pray for those who abuse you."*
Romans 12:14 *"Bless those who persecute you; bless and do not curse them."*

I regularly ask Muslims if I can pray for them before we part. Seldom do people refuse a prayer of blessing. I usually say something like, "How can I pray for you?" or "May I ask God to bless you and your family in these coming days?" or "Is there any need for which I could ask God to help you?" When people accept my offer, I tell them that I will pray to God in the name of Jesus because it is through Jesus that God answers our prayers.

> Purpose that you will not part with someone without offering to bless them or pray for them.

One time I prayed for a Muslim friend, and the Lord answered the prayer immediately. He couldn't stand up for twenty minutes because the power of God had come upon him. He said, "What have you done to me? I have never felt such a power in my life." He accepted the Lord a few weeks later. Many times I have seen people experience the power of God when we prayed with them or blessed them.

5. Pray with faith.

Romans 10:17 "*So faith comes from hearing, and hearing through the word of Christ.*"

James 5:15–16 "*And the prayer of faith will save the one who is sick, and the Lord will raise him up. And if he has committed sins, he will be forgiven. Therefore, confess your sins to one another and pray for one another, that you may be healed. The prayer of a righteous person has great power as it is working.*"

We once had a person who was strongly demonized. From one day to the next, he stopped speaking, eating, and was unable to move. He was like a dead person. We were not very experienced in casting out demons and especially not demons of this sort. We invited workers from many different denominations and backgrounds to come and pray. Everyone prayed in his own style, but we encouraged all to pray with faith that the Lord would deliver this man. We prayed for seven days, and the man was released from that demon. The way we pray is not nearly as significant as the persistence, frequency, and faith with which we pray.

6. Pray for men and women of peace.

Pray that the Lord would bring you in contact with men and women of peace. This expression of men and women of peace comes from Acts 10 where we read about Cornelius and Acts 16:13–15 where we read about Lydia. Men and women of peace are not just found by coincidence. The Lord of the harvest ordains godly appointments for us to meet those people, and prayer is a great way to find them.

7. Pray for your Timothy.

Jesus trained twelve disciples who later on brought the gospel to the world and started the amazing movement. He impacted them by teaching the Word to them, which changed their lives, and later on they taught the Word to others.

We know that Paul was advising Timothy to teach God's word to people who were able to train others.

2 Timothy 2:2 "*And what you have heard from me in the presence of many witnesses entrust to faithful men who will be able to teach others also.*"

Disciple others on your church planting team and among the new local believers. Seek out someone to disciple you.

CHALLENGE

Choose at least one of the following.

- Plan a time for daily prayer.

Monday	_____a.m./p.m.
Tuesday	_____a.m./p.m.
Wednesday	_____a.m./p.m.
Thursday	_____a.m./p.m.
Friday	_____a.m./p.m.
Saturday	_____a.m./p.m.
Sunday	_____a.m./p.m.

- Purpose that you will not part with someone without offering to bless them or pray for them. Recruit a strong team of prayer supporters. Ask God to show you people who will faithfully support you in prayer. Or send out an email asking for volunteers to be part of your prayer shield. Equip them monthly with prayer requests and praises and answered prayers. Write down the names of people you want to ask:

  _____

  _____

24

PROCLAMATION

The proclamation of the Word needs to be part of everything that we do. Radio ministries, TV shows, Facebook, evangelistic websites, chatting, evangelistic films, Bible distribution, and face-to-face talks are great ways to share the Word. The Word must reach people who have never had a chance to hear it.

1. Faith comes through the Word.

Romans 10:8–17 *"But what does it say? 'The word is near you, in your mouth and in your heart' (that is, the word of faith that we proclaim); because, if you confess with your mouth that Jesus is Lord and believe in your heart that God raised him from the dead, you will be saved. For with the heart one believes and is justified, and with the mouth one confesses and is saved. For the Scripture says, 'Everyone who believes in him will not be put to shame.' For there is no distinction between Jew and Greek; for the same Lord is Lord of all, bestowing his riches on all who call on him. For 'everyone who calls on the name of the Lord will be saved.' How then will they call on him in whom they have not believed? And how are they to believe in him of whom they have never heard? And how are they to hear without someone preaching? And how are they to preach unless they are sent? As it is written, 'How beautiful are the feet of those who preach the good news!' But they have not all obeyed the gospel. For Isaiah says, 'Lord, who has believed what he has heard from us?' So faith comes from hearing, and hearing through the word of Christ."*

Since faith only comes by the word of God, it is crucial to bring the word of God into every situation. The word of God is the most important thing we have to share. One very powerful tool, especially among Muslims, is to talk about Jesus, the Word made flesh, within the first five minutes of meeting someone. This lets people see that we love God and seek His ways in all areas of life. This often will bring us respect, and people may be more likely to come to us for advice or for prayer when they are in need. And we know that every word we sow by faith will not return void.

Isaiah 55:10–11 *"For as the rain and the snow come down from heaven and do not return there but water the earth, making it bring forth and sprout, giving seed to the sower and bread to the eater, so shall my word be that goes out from my mouth; it shall not return to me empty, but it shall accomplish that which I purpose, and shall succeed in the thing for which I sent it."*

We distributed a booklet with excerpts from Scripture and a plan of salvation to a Muslim tribe we were working with that was deeply involved in occult practices. The Lord guided me to present this booklet to one man who was fully covered with amulets and charms. A few weeks later I went back to see him and was surprised by what I saw. In the place of amulets and charms was a light on his face. When I asked him what had happened to him, he said, "The words in the booklet you gave me changed my life—I threw all the charms away and put my faith and trust in Jesus." Hallelujah! The word of God is powerful.

2. Our identity is in Jesus, therefore it is natural to speak about Him at all times.

We must be fully grounded in Jesus. A church planter needs to remind himself that he is first a citizen of heaven; this is his main identity. He is a businessman, an NGO worker, a teacher, a student, a house worker, etc. as a secondary role. If Jesus is our source of joy and love, and if He is the King and highest authority in our personal life, family life, and professional life, then it is normal for us to talk about Him in every situation.

Matthew 12:34 *"For out of the abundance of the heart the mouth speaks."*

While we need to be wise as well and ask the Holy Spirit when to speak and when to be silent, most church planters err on the side of not sharing Jesus enough. The Bible tells us to share the Word at all times.

2 Timothy 4:2 *"Preach the word; be ready in season and out of season; reprove, rebuke, and exhort, with complete patience and teaching."*

Sometimes people feel that they have to speak a language well before talking to people about Jesus. While I fully agree that long-term workers should master the heart language in which they want to minister, I also believe that people should share Jesus in the common trade language (English, French, etc.) from the day of their arrival.

3. Help others to proclaim the Word.

We need to teach local seekers and believers to obey the Word and to share it. When people start to obey the Word, they will grow in faith, and when they share the Word with others, the kingdom of God will advance and multiply.

One new believer came to Matthew 28:18–20 as he was reading the New Testament and asked me why it took Christians nearly two thousand years to bring the Word to his people. I asked him to forgive my ancestors and me for not obeying God's word and then challenged him to obey the word of God and share it with others even if it created problems in his life. He was silent as he considered my exhortation and then he said, "I will not be silent; I want to be obedient to God's word and share it with others, even if it costs my life."

4. Share the Word in the context of risk and suffering.

Sara and I were asked to do some counseling sessions for a group of people that had experienced a horrible burglary where one or two people were shot, but not killed. At the end of our counseling time, I felt the Holy Spirit lead me to ask them how they were sharing the word of Jesus with these needy, unreached peoples. Most of them were very surprised and told me that they could not do this because it would endanger their work in the country. I asked them if they believed that Jesus was the only way to be saved. Offering practical help brings temporary improvement to their lives, but those people will end up going to hell if they don't have a chance to hear about Jesus.

Before I moved to Africa, I was asked questions like, "How can you go and share the gospel in places where you know that you or the people you work with might be killed or put in prison when they accept Jesus? How can you take this responsibility?" Others have asked me how I could put my own children into situations where they might suffer persecution as a result of our family bringing Jesus to dark places. After I got out of prison, one person told me that he hoped I had learned my lesson and that I would do something else or share the gospel in areas where it was less dangerous.

The apostles shared the gospel in areas where persecution was common. Eleven of the twelve apostles were killed for the sake of sharing Jesus. It is normal to share Jesus in hostile environments because we believe that there is no other way for salvation.

Acts 4:12 *"And there is salvation in no one else, for there is no other name under heaven given among men by which we must be saved."*

Mark 8:34–38 *"And calling the crowd to him with his disciples, he said to them, 'If anyone would come after me, let him deny himself and take up his cross and follow me. For whoever would save his life will lose it, but whoever loses his life for my sake and the gospel's will save it. For what does it profit a man to gain the whole world and forfeit his soul? For what can a man give in return for his soul? For whoever is ashamed of me and of my words in this adulterous and sinful generation, of him will the Son of Man also be ashamed when he comes in the glory of his Father with the holy angels.'"*

> It is normal to share Jesus in hostile environments because we believe that there is no other way for salvation.

CHALLENGE

Choose at least one of the following.

- Set a goal to speak with five people about Jesus next month.

  _____

  _____

- Write out a commitment to the Lord that next month you will talk to three people about Jesus within the first five minutes of meeting them. Share your experience with a close friend.

  _____

  _____

25

PASSION & PURPOSE

What is your calling from God for your life? Has God given you a passion or purpose to advance His kingdom that drives your life? Often when God issues a calling for someone, it comes in stages. Maybe it starts with a lack of peace when you learn about a certain group of people that haven't heard the gospel. Unrest is often a sign that God is calling you to minister to those people in some way. The Lord rarely shows us the whole picture. Step by step, He reveals His plans to us so that we stay close to Him and walk by faith.

Ecclesiastes 3:11 *"He has made everything beautiful in its time. Also, he has put eternity into man's heart, yet so that he cannot find out what God has done from the beginning to the end."*

When I was in prison, the Lord put on my heart ten major blocks of people who represent the least reached groups of people in the world. While this list is not at all exhaustive, it is clear that these people need bold and courageous individuals to bring them the hope and salvation of Jesus. As you read this chapter, I pray that the Lord would stir in your heart a passion for one of these blocks of people and that you might dedicate your life to seeing Jesus glorified among them.

1. 1.5 billion Muslims

Muslims make up 21 percent of the world's population. Most Muslims are moderate. The fundamentalist Muslims that we hear about in the news represent a small minority. For example, when we had to leave our last country, many of our Muslim friends and neighbors cried and told us that they did not agree with what the government had done to us. However, both moderate and fundamentalist Muslims need to be introduced to Jesus.

2. One billion Hindus
Hinduism is the third-largest religion of the world after Christianity and Islam*. The majority of Hindus live in India. Even though some work has been done among them, large numbers of Hindus have never heard the gospel of Jesus Christ. Blinded by idol worship, they seek peace for their souls and place their hope in a cycle of reincarnation. For example, a Hindu believer might be disappointed with his current life or status in society. His hope is in the belief that if he lives well, he might have higher societal status in his next life. Who will bring the peace of Jesus to the many unreached Hindu castes?

3. Nearly 500 million Buddhists
Buddhists don't believe in a God who created the world, and they don't believe that God rules the world. They see life as a journey that ends by returning to the earth. Who will bring the eternal hope of Jesus to the Buddhists so that they will know about their creator God and will receive eternal life through Jesus Christ?

4. The Western world
Historically, Europe was one of the homelands of Christianity, and from there it spread to North America, Africa, and Asia. Materialism, drugs, homosexuality, alcoholism and other idols have replaced the true God, and people have become more concerned with pleasing themselves and men than with pleasing God. Europeans are becoming disillusioned with a lifestyle that hopes in money and self-gratification. May God raise up passionate Christ followers who obey the teaching of Jesus in every area of their lives to reach out in their communities and even in the traditional churches.

5. The poor all over the world
Poverty is a problem that can never be fully solved, and attempting to solve it, even in part, can be overwhelming. Jesus himself reminds us that we will always have the poor with us in Matthew 26:11. As we consider ways to serve

the poor practically and ease their suffering on this earth, let us not forget that they will experience eternal suffering without the truth of the gospel.

6. Children and youth

Based on a survey taken in the USA, people age thirteen or younger have the highest probability of accepting the gospel. It is a general principle that younger people accept the Lord more readily than older people. We need to focus on reaching younger people with the gospel.

I traveled on a train in West Africa and sat next to an older man. He was a devoted follower of Islam. During the twenty hours we had together, we both shared our faith with each other. When this old man heard about the assurance of salvation and the sacrifice of Jesus he told me, "If what you say is true, then your way is better than my way! Please come to my village and tell my children and my grandchildren about this because they need to hear this good news." When I asked him if he wanted to follow Jesus and receive forgiveness of sins, he said, "I am too old. I have lived my whole life this way. I cannot accept this Jesus, but my children and grandchildren can. Please come to my village and share Jesus with them."

7. Women, roughly half of the world's population

In certain Eastern communities and countries, women are much more difficult to reach with the gospel. Some very rarely leave their houses, and others are told that religion is not for women and that they should just follow their husbands or families without thinking about religious issues. When women meet Jesus, they often face more challenges than men do. In many societies, women are the main influencers of the next generation. If they are reached with the gospel, they have great potential to strongly impact the future.

8. Millions of business people

These precious men and women in high-power positions in the business world are often very lonely. Business people often struggle with the many responsibilities they have and are often overwhelmed. They usually do not have many people with whom they can share their burdens. They need people who can share their burdens and introduce them to Jesus, the ultimate burden bearer.

9. Millions of athletes and their fans

People of all ages either participate in sports, support sporting activities, or watch sports in their free time. We can reach out with the gospel to our teammates if we play a sport or by inviting friends to watch a game in our homes on TV if we do not. Most nations have their traditional or national sports and love to talk about them. Sports are a great way to bring Jesus to millions who have never heard the gospel.

10. The political world

Authentic Christians who work in this world can have great influence on other politicians by bringing Jesus and biblical values into this arena.

1 Timothy 2:1–2 *"I urge that supplications, prayers, intercessions, and thanksgivings be made for all people, for kings and all who are in high positions, that we may lead a peaceful and quiet life, godly and dignified in every way."*

Rulers and people in power have a lot of influence over the spread of the gospel. It is clear that the Lord wants to bring some Christians who are willing to stand up for Him into positions of influence and authority, and he wants other Christians to pray for them.

CHALLENGE

Choose at least one of the following.

* Commit to praying every day for a month for one of the following groups. Circle the one you feel drawn to pray for.

Muslims	The Western World	Women
Hindus	The Poor	The Business World
Buddhists	Children and Youth	Sports Fans
Politicians	Other:	

- As you read about these different blocks of people, was your heart stirred for any of them? Write down one thing you can do to reach out to or serve one of these groups:

  _____

  _____

  _____

- Is God asking you to make a major change in your life so that you can bring the gospel to one of these groups?

Change jobs:

_____

Move to a new city:

_____

Move to a new country:

_____

Change the way you spend your free time:

_____

Other:

_____

26

POWER

Your denomination and theological background are irrelevant. We need the power of God if we want to be successful church planters among unreached peoples. We will face many challenging situations as we enter a land that has been in the enemy's hands for decades or often hundreds of years. In my experience, most people experience the power of the Holy Spirit only if they are willing and seek it with all their hearts. God wants to glorify His own name by confirming His word through signs, wonders, dreams, healings, the casting out of demons, and other supernatural deeds done by the Holy Spirit.

As the disciples came together and prayed fervently for God's power to be released in their ministry, we also must pray for God's amazing outpouring of His power. We can never have enough of God, and we must desire more of Him as the deer pants for water.

> We can never have enough of God, and we must desire more of Him as the deer pants for water.

1. God's power makes us bold.

Acts 4:29–30 "*And now, Lord, stretch out your hand to heal, and signs and wonders are performed through the name of your holy servant Jesus. And when they had prayed, the place in which they were gathered together was shaken, and they were all filled with the Holy Spirit and continued to speak the word of God with boldness.*"

When the power of God comes upon us, we will be filled with the Holy Spirit to speak the Word boldly. The Pharisees were amazed at how the disciples spoke the word of God fearlessly. The people who killed Steven were astonished to see him speak the truth boldly even when he faced death.

2. God's power will manifest in all kinds of miracles.

The ministry of Jesus was always based on the Word, and it was often accompanied by signs and wonders. When Jesus was asked by John the Baptist whether He was the one to come or if they should wait for another, He answered with the following:

Luke 7: 22 *"Go and tell John what you have seen and heard: the blind receive their sight, the lame walk, lepers are cleansed, and the deaf hear, the dead are raised up, the poor have good news preached to them."*

Paul describes his ministry by pointing out what Jesus accomplished through him in word and deed and the power of God through signs and wonders.

Romans 15:18–19 *"For I will not venture to speak of anything except what Christ has accomplished through me to bring the Gentiles to obedience—by word and deed, by the power of signs and wonders, by the power of the Spirit of God—so that from Jerusalem and all the way around to Illyricum I have fulfilled the ministry of the gospel of Christ."*

Signs and wonders do not save people. Many witnessed signs and miracles in the lives of Jesus and Paul, but didn't surrender their lives to God. However, Romans 15 says that by word and deed the Gentiles were brought to obedience of the gospel. While signs and wonders never produce faith, they often produce openness for the gospel because, through them, people experience and see God's power.

3. The kingdom of God is a kingdom of power.

1 Corinthians 2:4–5 *"and my speech and my message were not in plausible words of wisdom, but in demonstration of the Spirit and of power, so that your faith might not rest in the wisdom of men but in the power of God."*

We enter the kingdom of God by His power. Whenever a person finds Jesus, it is always the power of God that has opened his heart and his mind. The Pharisees taught Scripture using human arguments. Jesus used the Scripture with authority and the power of God made the words alive.

Matthew 7:28–29 *"And when Jesus finished these sayings, the crowds were astonished at his teaching, for he was teaching them as one who had authority, and not as their scribes."*

Paul also used the Scriptures with God's authority and power when he spoke.

1 Corinthians 4:19–20 *"But I will come to you soon, if the Lord wills, and I will find out not the talk of these arrogant people but their power. For the Kingdom of God does not consist in talk but in power."*

1 Thessalonians 1:5 *"because our gospel came to you not only in word, but also in power and in the Holy Spirit and with full conviction."*

4. God's power is released through praying and fasting.

We read in Scripture that praying, often accompanied by fasting, releases God's power. For example, certain demons can only be cast out with prayer and fasting.

Mark 9:29 *"This kind can come out only by prayer and fasting."* (ISV)

We saw a man delivered from evil spirits through our prayer and fasting during our time in Africa. He had received a copy of the New Testament from a friend of his and surrendered his life to Jesus. The next day, he started behaving very strangely. He stopped eating, drinking, and talking. After some time praying and fasting, the demons manifested and said, "We will never leave this man. He belongs to us and the whole region where he comes from belongs to us." Then the demons were quiet again. We proclaimed God's truth and said that this man and the area from which he came belonged to Jesus. After a while, the person was released and started to drink water. Then he danced and rejoiced because Jesus had set him free.

5. God's power is needed because our battle exists in the invisible world.

Christians who grew up in the West don't have as much experience regarding the unseen spiritual world as Christians who grew up in Asia or Africa. When I was in Asia teaching a group of believers, I visited a local mosque with one of the believers. On the way into the mosque, we walked through an area that looked like a market. As we entered the mosque, I saw something I would not have believed had I not see it with my own eyes. Dozens of men and women were writhing around on the floor and hanging from the trees. They all were fully demonized. Some had foam coming out of their mouths, and others flailed in ways that should have been impossible without severe injury. It was just awful to see the power of the devil manifested in these precious people. It is clear in the Bible that our fight is not against flesh and blood, but against the rulers and powers of darkness.

Ephesians 6:12 *"For we do not wrestle against flesh and blood, but against the rulers, against the authorities, against the cosmic powers over this present darkness, against the spiritual forces of evil in the heavenly places."*

While it is good to be aware of this battle, we also have no reason to fear it. We should engage in this battle with the powers of darkness, knowing that we are on the winning side because Jesus has already achieved the victory on the cross.

Colossians 2:15 *"He disarmed the rulers and authorities and put them to open shame, by triumphing over them in him."*

6. God's power provokes power encounters with the kingdom of darkness.

Wherever Jesus showed up, the powers of the darkness manifested in people because they were threatened by the power of God. There are indeed two kingdoms clashing together, the kingdom of light and the kingdom of darkness. When a Spirit-filled person threatens the powers of darkness, they will have to manifest, and it often ends in a power encounter that reveals that God's power is superior to the power of darkness.

Mark 5:2.6–7 *"And when Jesus had stepped out of the boat, immediately there met him out of the tombs a man with an unclean spirit. And when he saw Jesus from afar, he ran and fell down before him. And crying out with a loud voice, he said, 'What have you to do with me, Jesus, Son of the Most High God? I adjure you by God, do not torment me.'"*

Acts 16:17–18 *"She would follow Paul and us and shout, 'These men are servants of the Most High God and are proclaiming to you a way of salvation!' She kept doing this for many days until Paul became annoyed, turned to her and told the spirit, 'I command you in the name of Jesus the Messiah to come out of her!' And it came out that very moment."*

Once, while sharing the gospel with a group of Muslims in Asia, we sensed a great openness, and indeed, many wanted to follow Jesus. But one person started to behave and growl like a tiger. Speaking in the language of the people, he said to us, "I will kill you white men. You and your friend will stop talking about Jesus." Since we did not understand what the man was saying, we just kept standing there, but the people around us ran away. The demon-possessed person ran towards us. We began to pray and he fell down like a dead person. A few minutes later he stood up delivered.

Most unreached tribes in the world today are involved in occult practices, even if they subscribe to one of the major world religions. The task is to reach these precious people with the good news and the power of the gospel manifested by the work of the Holy Spirit so that they will be released from the power of darkness.

CHALLENGE

Choose at least one of the following.

- Take some time to fast and pray for God to increase His power in your life.

- Get in the habit of fasting weekly or monthly. Choose one day of the week or a certain time during the month for your regular fast.

- Ask the Lord if there is anything in your heart or life that might prevent the free flow of His power and then spend some time listening and waiting for His answer.

_____

_____

_____

27

PERSEVERANCE

The Bible often speaks about the importance of patience, endurance, and perseverance. In this decade of high speed Internet and easy worldwide travel, we need to learn the lessons of patience and perseverance from those who have run the race before us. When people left their home country to reach unreached tribes in Africa or Asia a hundred years ago, they did not expect to come back. They were fully committed and willing to persevere until a church was planted or until their death.

1. Perseverance will bless you personally.

James 5:11 *"Behold, we consider those blessed who remained steadfast. You have heard of the steadfastness of Job, and you have seen the purpose of the Lord, how the Lord is compassionate and merciful."*

Job 42:10 *"And the LORD restored the fortunes of Job, when he had prayed for his friends. And the LORD gave Job twice as much as he had before."*

Through endurance and patience, Abraham had a son with Sarah, and through him God blessed all the nations. Through his grandchildren came Jesus Christ, the Savior of the world, so he indeed became a blessing for all the nations. After a painful and long wait, God gave Hannah a son, Samuel, one of the greatest prophets in history. We could add many other biblical examples of patience and endurance that resulted in enormous blessing. Through the examples of Job, Abraham, and Hannah, we understand that perseverance and patience will produce a great blessing for the one who endures.

2. Perseverance will make you mature and complete in your walk with God.

James. 1:2–4 "*Count it all joy, my brothers, when you meet trials of various kinds, for you know that the testing of your faith produces steadfastness. And let steadfastness have its full effect, that you may be perfect and complete, lacking in nothing.*"

It is our Lord's greatest desire to see his people mature and grow in faith so that He may be most glorified through us. Jesus expresses this in John 15 where He uses the example of the vine. The branches in our lives that don't bear fruit are pruned through trials and challenging situations. The closer we walk with the Lord, the more he can refine us. Abraham experienced what might be one of the most difficult trials a person can experience. When God commanded Abraham to sacrifice his son, He tested Abraham's faith to make it mature and complete so he would not lack anything.

3. Persevere in troubles because of the joy set before you.

Romans 12:12 "*Rejoice in hope, be patient in tribulation, be constant in prayer.*"
Romans 5:2 ". . . *we rejoice in the hope of the glory of God.*"

A believer has hope that he will see the glory of God one day face to face, and this is a constant source of joy in whatever situation he might face in life.

Romans 5:5 "*And hope does not put us to shame, because God's love has been poured into our hearts through the Holy Spirit who has been given to us.*"

In challenging situations, the devil wants to take away the hope of the glory of God. Therefore, we are encouraged to be patient in trouble and to persist in prayer. Through perseverance and persistent prayer, one can keep on rejoicing in the glory of God whatever situation he might face in life because he knows that this hope will never disappoint us.

4. Persevere in your vision.

Romans 8:25 "*But if we hope for what we do not see, we wait for it with patience.*"
Proverbs 29:18 "*Where there is no prophetic vision the people cast off restraint.*"

A church planter, especially one in a pioneering situation, needs to be fully devoted to the vision that the Holy Spirit has given him, even if in the natural sphere, he does not see anything at all. This will help him to wait with patience and eager expectation for its fulfillment in the visible world. A church planter without vision can "perish" or give up his job and do something else.

5. Perseverance leads to harvest.

Galatians 6:9 *"And let us not grow weary of doing good, for in due season we will reap, if we do not give up."*

1 Corinthians 15:58 *"Therefore, my beloved brothers, be steadfast, immovable, always abounding in the work of the Lord, knowing that in the Lord your labor is not in vain."*

Today, more than ever before in history, we see much more fruit among unreached tribes, even Muslim tribes, all over the world. We live in an exciting time as we believe that the end of the world is drawing near, and we have the promise that the Lord will pour out more of his Spirit (Joel 2). According to Garrison, during the twentieth century, there had been ten movements of Muslim communities to faith in Jesus. Garrison continues,

> In the first 12 years of the 21st century an additional 64 movements of Muslims to Christ have appeared. These 21st-century movements are not isolated to one or two corners of the world. They are taking place across the Muslim world: in sub-Saharan Africa, in the Persian world, in the Arab world, in Turkestan, in South Asia and in Southeast Asia. Something is happening, something historic, something unprecedented.[2]

Sooner or later the harvest will be ready in every field. The Bible encourages us not to get tired, but to faithfully do the work the Lord has called us to do. If we are steadfast and excel in the work of the Lord, we can be 100% sure that nothing we do will be wasted.

---

2   David Garrison, "God is Doing Something Historic," *Mission Frontiers* 35, no. 4 (2013): 6–9.

CHALLENGE

Choose at least one of the following.

- Is there a trial or challenging situation that you are facing right now? Ask God to produce perseverance and patience in your character through it.

- Ask the Lord to show you His vision and His dreams for the people with whom you work. Ask Him for the ability to see in the Spirit what is not yet seen in the natural world, and then persevere until it comes to fruition.

_____

_____

_____

28

PERSECUTION

Be ready to be persecuted.

1. Suffering is promised for every believer.
2 Timothy 3:12 "*Indeed, all who desire to live a godly life in Christ Jesus will be persecuted.*"

Some are mocked at school or work because they stand up for Jesus, and others lose their jobs or some of their possessions because of Him. Some are imprisoned for their faith, while others are separated from family and friends. Others face physical torture or death. No matter what kind of persecution we face, we know that the Lord will never leave us alone in our suffering.

1 Peter 4:12 "*Beloved, do not be surprised at the fiery trial when it comes upon you to test you, as though something strange were happening to you.*"

Peter reminds us that persecution should not be a surprise to us. This means we should actually prepare for it as much as we can. We prepare for many things in life: our studies, work, sports, etc. As Christians, and especially as church planters among unreached peoples, we need to prepare ourselves, our marriages, our families, our teams, and our extended community for persecution. The question is not if persecution will come, but when.

We need to be very practical when we speak about preparing for suffering. The Bible tells us to count the costs before building a house so that we will not be ashamed in the process if we cannot finish it. When Father Zakaria Botros was asked how he could live knowing there was a $1,000,000 bounty for his head, he answered, "The day the Lord called me to this ministry, I died; every day since has just been His grace."

Romans 6:4 "*We were buried therefore with him by baptism into death, in order that, just as Christ was raised from the dead by the glory of the Father, we too might walk in newness of life.*"

We can also prepare with our spouses by speaking and praying about it so that when suffering comes, it will be easier to deal with. Read your kids biographies of cross-cultural workers to prepare them for the suffering of their parents or even for their own suffering. The Trailblazer series for children has been a blessing for our family.

My son read many of these biographies, and one day he said, "In all the biographies I read, the men or women were either in prison, tortured, or even killed. You haven't experienced any of this—are you a missionary?" What great understanding my son got through these books! The stories of these saints made it clear to him that a missionary must be ready to suffer for Christ.

A team needs to make persecution a topic as well so that the members of the team know how to act when one member faces persecution. For example, the team leader might openly stand behind the person or couple who is under persecution, while the rest of the

> "The day the Lord called me to this ministry, I died; every day since has just been His grace."

team separates from the situation to avoid the possibility of expulsion. Or the whole team might decide to stand fully behind anyone who faces persecution. People need to know how to act when persecution comes.

2. Rejoice in your sufferings.

Romans 5:3–5 "*Not only that, but we rejoice in our sufferings, knowing that suffering produces endurance, and endurance produces character, and character produces hope, and hope does not put us to shame, because God's love has been poured into our hearts through the Holy Spirit who has been given to us.*"

James 1:2–3 "*Count it all joy, my brothers, when you meet trials of various kinds, for you know that the testing of your faith produces steadfastness.*"

Romans 8:28 "*And we know that for those who love God all things work together for good, for those who are called according to his purpose.*"

Remind yourself that all things are working together for good for those who love God, therefore rejoice in the Lord at all times.

3. Suffering fills up what is lacking in Christ's afflictions.

Colossians 1:24 *"Now I rejoice in my sufferings for your sake, and in my flesh I am filling up what is lacking in Christ's afflictions for the sake of his body, that is, the church."*

It is very clear theologically that one cannot add anything to Christ's afflictions. Jesus completed the work of salvation at the cross. When Paul speaks about the "lack" in Christ's afflictions, he is referring to his personal suffering as a church planter as a demonstration in the flesh to unbelievers of the suffering that Christ endured for them.

4. If you are suffering, then you are blessed by God.

1 Peter 4:14 *"If you are insulted for the name of Christ, you are blessed, because the Spirit of glory and of God rests upon you."*

Matthew 5:11 *"Blessed are you when others revile you and persecute you and utter all kinds of evil against you falsely on my account."*

1 Peter 3:14 *"But even if you should suffer for righteousness' sake, you will be blessed. Have no fear of them, nor be troubled."*

We all like to be blessed and bless others. The Bible says that suffering is a blessing, but often we don't think like this when we think about suffering. Why is suffering considered to be a blessing? One of the reasons we see in the Scriptures above is that suffering for Christ is a sign that the glorious spirit of God is resting on us. Persecution makes a person either better or bitter. We need to have a humble heart, fully depending on Jesus so that suffering will indeed be a blessing for us and not a reason to abandon faith.

> Persecution makes a person either better or bitter.

5. Don't feel ashamed when you suffer for Christ.

1 Peter 4:16 *"Yet if anyone suffers as a Christian, let him not be ashamed, but let him glorify God in that name."*

2 Timothy 1:8 *"Therefore do not be ashamed of the testimony about our Lord, nor of me his prisoner, but share in suffering for the gospel by the power of God."*

When we suffer for Jesus, we bring glory to his name, not shame. We must overcome any shame in our hearts and share this truth with new believers who are often accused of betraying their families and therefore bringing shame on them. Suffering for Jesus is not a reason to be ashamed before God, even if we experience shame before men.

6. Bless those who persecute you and continue to do good.

Romans 12:14 *"Bless those who persecute you; bless and do not curse them."*

1 Peter 4:19 *"Therefore let those who suffer according to God's will entrust their souls to a faithful Creator while doing good."*

The power of love and forgiveness in action helps suffering Christians to bless their persecutors. It is only through the closeness of Jesus and the sweet fellowship of the Holy Spirit that one can bless his enemies and continue to do good. As church planters, we need to be prepared to bless our enemies in whatever situation we find ourselves. Remember, we are not fighting against flesh and blood, but against the evil spirits that lead those who don't know Jesus.

Ephesians 6:12 *"For we do not wrestle against flesh and blood, but against the rulers, against the authorities, against the cosmic powers over this present darkness, against the spiritual forces of evil in the heavenly places."*

When we meet our persecutors face to face, we need to pray that God helps us to see them as people who know not what they are doing and who deeply need Jesus.

7. Suffering will help you to comfort others.

2 Corinthians 1:3–4 *"Blessed be the God and Father of our Lord Jesus Christ, the Father of mercies and God of all comfort, who comforts us in all our affliction, so that we may be able to comfort those who are in any affliction, with the comfort with which we ourselves are comforted by God."*

God often allows something to happen to you so that you can learn and then bless others through your experience. When the Lord allows you to suffer for His name, He wants you to use this blessing to serve and comfort others who might face similar situations.

8. Suffering for Christ is considered to be a privilege.

Philippians 1:29 *"For it has been granted to you that for the sake of Christ you should not only believe in him but also suffer for his sake."*

I often reflect on the privilege I have in knowing Jesus, a privilege so many millions of people around me do not have. But this verse goes further and speaks not only about those who have the privilege of knowing Jesus, but also about the honor of suffering for him.

A friend of mine suffered such terrible torture that, humanly speaking, he actually should not have survived. I had the privilege of seeing him and hearing his testimony a few days after he was miraculously released. The joy of Jesus he reflected, the presence of Jesus on his face, and the sweet fellowship of the Holy Spirit in his life made many of us realize how privileged he was to suffer for Christ and to experience supernatural closeness with Jesus.

Remember to be joyful whenever you face persecution. How do you prepare yourself, your family, and your team for persecution? Suffering is a privilege; therefore, rejoice in it.

CHALLENGE

Choose at least one of the following.

- Talk about possible persecution with your spouse and kids.

- Make a plan as a team that describes clearly how you will handle potential situations.

- Testify to someone about a time when you suffered for His sake and thank God for the blessings that came from that suffering.

29

PROXIMATE BELIEVERS

God has provided millions of workers who are proximate to unreached peoples to bring in His harvest. Proximate believers are people who are from a reached people group but often speak the same language, have the same culture, and/or live in the same country or city with the unreached peoples. While they are close culturally or linguistically to the unreached peoples, tribal barriers prevent the gospel from being spread from the believing tribe to the unreached tribes. Many of these proximate believers have lived among unreached peoples for years or decades without seeing themselves as potential church planters. In many places around the world, people are stuck in the thinking that church planters need to be full-time pastors or evangelists. However, we must remember that all believers are part of the general priesthood.

1 Peter 2:9 *"But you are a chosen race, a royal priesthood, a holy nation, a people for his own possession, that you may proclaim the excellencies of him who called you out of darkness into his marvelous light."*

The understanding that every believer is part of the priesthood has the potential to mobilize thousands of church planters. What is generally needed is simple training about cross-cultural ministry, including topics like sharing the gospel in a relevant way, discipleship issues, house churches, and multiplication. A good reference on this topic is *And You Shall Be a Blessing* by Ben Naja and Mussa Sy.[3]

---

3   Ben Naja and Mussa Sy, *And You Shall Be a Blessing: Encountering People of Other Cultures and Religions* (VTR Publications, 2011).

God's mighty work in the Global South

In 1960, about 75 percent of all born again Christians lived in the Global North, which is Europe and North America. Today, at least 75 percent of the evangelical Christians live in the Global South, which is Asia, Africa, and South America. The Holy Spirit has done a mighty work in these unreached areas where the gospel wasn't present for hundreds of years. God has changed the image of Christianity in the world within the last fifty years, and those who were last have become first.

Matthew 20:16 "*So the last will be first, and the first last.*"

Isaiah prophesied in 52:15 and Paul confirmed it in Romans 15:21: "*Those who have never been told of him will see, and those who have never heard will understand.*"

The local church as God's presence in that place

God told Joshua:

Joshua 1:3 "*Every place that the sole of your foot will tread upon I have given to you, just as I promised to Moses.*"

The Israelites represented the kingdom of God on earth at that time. It was important for Joshua to put his foot on the land in order to possess it.

Paul says that the church represents the fullness of the visible presence of Christ's body on earth today.

Ephesians 1:22–23 "*And he put all things under his feet and gave him as head over all things to the church, which is his body, the fullness of him who fills all in all.*"

Ephesians 3:10 "*So that through the church the manifold wisdom of God might now be made known to the rulers and authorities in the heavenly places.*"

The church represents God's manifold wisdom before the rulers and authorities in the heavenly places. We should therefore never neglect the church in a given place.

> Wherever there is a church, it represents Christ's body, and Jesus is the head of it. The church is a light in the midst of darkness.

Global South workers and workers from the West finishing the task together

The task that we received from Jesus in what is commonly referred to as the Great Commission is a big assignment. If the task is to be finished soon, we need a lot of workers who are willing to take the gospel to a new culture.

Matthew 9:37–38 "*The harvest is plentiful, but the laborers are few; therefore pray earnestly to the Lord of the harvest to send out laborers into his harvest.*"

Western missionaries and Christians from the Global South working together will be able to finish the task. Each culture brings a unique strength to the table. I personally have been blessed to see the special anointing in prayer in my Korean colleagues; the wisdom and experience of house church movements in my Chinese colleagues; and the experience in casting out demons in some of my African colleagues. As a Westerner, I have experienced the treasure of a heritage of a long church history. God wants to use workers from all places to bring the gospel to the last unreached peoples in the world.

Adapted sending structures for movements from the Global South

Often, strong and fruitful Christians live in close proximity with unreached people groups, but outreach does not naturally happen. These Christians often need to be trained and mobilized to reach out to neighboring, unreached peoples. Paul's style of tent-making, working in your profession while being intentional about sharing the gospel, is a very effective way for Christians in the Global South to spread the good news of the kingdom.

I know of one situation where a denomination of churches existed for about fifty years next to dozens of unreached people groups. In four years, with some training and prayer, this denomination sent more than eighty workers to work in their profession and live among these nearby, unreached people groups.

Releasing the Workers of the Eleventh Hour: The Global South and the Task Remaining by Ben Naja is a great book for those who are interested in learning more.[4]

---

4   Ben Naja, *Releasing the Workers of the Eleventh Hour: The Global South and the Task Remaining* (Pasadena: William Carey Library, 2008).

Church-based teams reaching unreached peoples

Through globalization the world became a village. We often have Christians and unreached peoples living together in the same city or area. Because of cultural differences, these unreached peoples often have little or no interaction with the Christians. The Christians must exert a special effort to start teams that have the vision to do cross-cultural ministry and bring the good news to the unreached peoples among them.

During a training seminar that I led for about a hundred pastors and church leaders in Nairobi, Kenya, I asked them to raise their hands if their church had a ministry for certain types of people. When I listed common church ministries such as weekly Bible studies, prayer, women's groups, youth ministry, and choir, almost everyone raised their hands. However, not one person raised a hand when I asked them about a ministry that included cross-cultural outreach to the unreached Muslims in their cities. Afterwards, some of the leaders approached me and said, "This will change now—we need to start church based teams that will reach out to these unreached peoples."

CHALLENGE

Choose at least one of the following.

- Pray for church leaders in your city. Visit them and share your burden for the unreached with them.

- Pray and invest part of your time to train and equip proximate believers, and you will multiply your church planting efforts.

30

PRESENCE IN A COMMUNITY

Jesus himself spent three years with the twelve men He called to follow Him. He spent time with them, shared life with them, and appointed them to be the apostles who took the good news all over the world.

1. Jesus, our example to follow

Jesus is our example; He showed us what it means to live among the people He wanted to reach. He left heaven and decided to live among us so that we could see Him, touch Him, and hear Him.

Philippians 2:5–8 *"Have this mind among yourselves, which is yours in Christ Jesus, who, though he was in the form of God, did not count equality with God a thing to be grasped, but emptied himself, by taking the form of a servant, being born in the likeness of men. And being found in human form, he humbled himself by becoming obedient to the point of death, even death on a cross."*

1 John 1:1 *"That which was from the beginning, which we have heard, which we have seen with our eyes, which we looked upon and have touched with our hands, concerning the word of life . . ."*

We can live among the people we want to reach and give them the chance not just to hear the message, but also to see it, touch it, and experience it. We are Christ's living letter.

2 Corinthians 3:2–3 *"You yourselves are our letter of recommendation, written on our hearts, to be known and read by all. And you show that you are a letter*

from Christ delivered by us, written not with ink but with the Spirit of the living God, not on tablets of stone but on tablets of human hearts."

2. Paul's cross-cultural ministry

1 Corinthians 9:19–23 *"For though I am free from all, I have made myself a servant to all, that I might win more of them. To the Jews I became as a Jew, in order to win Jews. To those under the law I became as one under the law (though not being myself under the law) that I might win those under the law. To those outside the law I became as one outside the law (not being outside the law of God but under the law of Christ) that I might win those outside the law. To the weak I became weak, that I might* win the weak. I have become all things to all people, that by all means I might save some. I do it all for the sake of the gospel, that I may share with them in its blessings."

> The only motivation for contextualization must be the winning of souls.

Paul was a free man, made free through Christ Jesus, but he made himself a servant to the people he served to win people for Christ. The only motivation for contextualization* must be the winning of souls. Our lives should not preach any other message but Jesus to the community we want to reach.

1 Corinthians 2:2 *"For I decided to know nothing among you except Jesus Christ and him crucified."*

3. Be friendly—be good news

When you enter a community to win them for Christ, be friendly. Small things can open doors to win people's hearts.

John 4:7 *"A woman from Samaria came to draw water. Jesus said to her, 'Give me a drink.'"*

Acts 17:22 *"So Paul, standing in the midst of the Areopagus, said: 'Men of Athens, I perceive that in every way you are very religious.'"*

Acts 18:2–3 *". . . And he went to see them, and because he was of the same trade he stayed with them and worked, for they were tentmakers by trade."*

Be good news and bring good news to the people. Do not attack their culture or their behavior; rather, look for and affirm strengths in the culture and then share Jesus as good news with them.

4. Be a blessing to the community

Whatever you can do to bless the community—do it. This is part of the gospel. Share the love of Jesus practically.

James 4:17 *"So whoever knows the right thing to do and fails to do it, for him it is sin."*

NGO work, business, education, and healthcare are examples of great ways to be part of a community. Some might go into a community and bring the blessing of Jesus through the signs of the kingdom by preaching the gospel, healing the sick, and casting out demons. The blessing of signs and wonders often goes together with the practical deeds of love and service in the community.

Luke 10:8–9 *"Whenever you enter a town and they receive you, eat what is set before you. Heal the sick in it and say to them, 'The Kingdom of God has come near to you.'"*

5. Bring Jesus into communities and see them transformed

John 4:28–29 and 4:40–42 *"So the woman left her water jar and went away into town and said to the people, 'Come, see a man who told me all that I ever did. Can this be the Christ?' So when the Samaritans came to him, they asked him to stay with them, and he stayed there two days. And many more believed because of his word. They said to the woman, 'It is no longer because of what you said that we believe, for we have heard for ourselves, and we know that this is indeed the Savior of the world.'"*

Jesus entered into the Samaritan woman's community, and part of her village was saved. Peter met Cornelius, and through him, his extended family was saved (Acts 10). Paul's relationships with Lydia and the prison guard resulted in both of their extended families entering the kingdom (Acts 16:11–15, 22–34).

How can you be present in the community you want to reach? How can you bring good news to them?

Challenge
Choose at least one of the following.

• List some of the positive attributes of your host culture.

_____

_____

_____

• What are some practical ways to bless and serve the communities that you want to reach with the gospel?

_____

_____

_____

31

PARTNERSHIP

When we partner with others, we recognize that we don't have all the gifts and resources needed in and of ourselves, and the unity and interdependence that results reveals God's love to the world.

Romans 12:4–5 *"For as in one body we have many members, and the members do not all have the same function, so we, though many, are one body in Christ, and individually members one of another."*

John 13:35 *"By this all people will know that you are my disciples, if you have love for one another."*

1. The Trinity

Our first and most important partner is God who wants to guide us in His work through the Holy Spirit who lives in us. He will help us in prayer, reveal His plans to us, and lead us in all truth. He is our main partner in all we do.

Romans 8:26 *"Likewise the Spirit helps us in our weakness. For we do not know what to pray for as we ought, but the Spirit himself intercedes for us with groanings too deep for words."*

Amos 3:7 *"For the Lord GOD does nothing without revealing his secret to his servants the prophets."*

John 15:5 *"I am the vine; you are the branches. Whoever abides in me and I in him, he it is that bears much fruit, for apart from me you can do nothing."*

John 16:13 *"When the Spirit of truth comes, he will guide you into all the truth ..."*

2. Ministry partner

By "ministry partner," I am referring to your spouse if you are married or to a solid, same-gender friendship if you are single. These relationships are crucial if we want to last on the field.

Galatians 6:2 "*Bear one another's burdens, and so fulfill the law of Christ.*"

It is absolutely essential to live out this verse in a practical way. Have regular times together to pray and carry each other's burdens.

3. Family

While each family member has a different role, it is very important that everyone in the family feels the call for the ministry that the family is doing.

Our experience has been that the Lord often opened doors to enter new communities through our children. Children are a blessing from God and are part of the ministry God has entrusted to you.

> Children are a blessing from God and are part of the ministry God has entrusted to you.

Spend time with your family and respect the Sabbath day so that you can focus on and influence your children. By spending time with your children, you are raising up the next generation of church planters.

Deuteronomy 6:7 "*You shall teach them diligently to your children, and shall talk of them when you sit in your house, and when you walk by the way, and when you lie down, and when you rise.*"

Psalm 78:5 "*He established a testimony in Jacob and appointed a law in Israel, which he commanded our fathers to teach to their children.*"

4. Team

Jesus had a team of twelve disciples with whom he was doing the ministry. Later on Jesus sent the seventy-two disciples two by two. Paul and Barnabas first worked together, and then each of them continued with his own team. Church planting and advancing the kingdom of God are team activities.

Ecclesiastes 4:9–12 "*Two are better than one, because they have a good reward for their toil. For if they fall, one will lift up his fellow. But woe to him who is alone when he falls and has not another to lift him up! Again, if two lie together, they keep warm, but how can one keep warm alone? And though a man might prevail against one who is alone, two will withstand him—a threefold cord is not quickly broken.*"

5. God's team

Often a variety of denominations and sending entities have workers in the same city with the same goal to reach a certain people group. These workers are commonly referred to as "God's Team." We must work together and nurture these relationships even if there are differences in strategy or theology. Regular prayer times and meetings to discuss general strategy can be incredibly beneficial for not only the workers themselves but also the people among whom they live.

Psalm 133:1–3 *"Behold, how good and pleasant it is when brothers dwell in unity! It is like the precious oil on the head, running down on the beard, on the beard of Aaron, running down on the collar of his robes! It is like the dew of Hermon, which falls on the mountains of Zion! For there the* LORD *has commanded the blessing, life forevermore."*

6. The local church

We spoke about the proximate believers before. Let me just emphasize again that the local church is God's presence in that place. Do not neglect it. Instead, partner with it.

Two beautiful local brothers were willing, without hesitation, to be my guarantors so that I could leave the country, knowing that they could face prison and fines if I did not return. The local church is a blessing to you, and you can be a blessing to them.

7. Larger community around the world

Partner with the larger community. Share your prayer requests with them regularly, and inform them about the work. Let them be part of the joy of building the kingdom of God among unreached peoples from afar by praying, giving, and sending people to serve.

Before I was released from prison, people from all over the world were praying and fasting for it. When I was miraculously released on the second day of prayer and fasting, people all over the world rejoiced with me. We are indeed one body in Christ.

CHALLENGE

Choose at least one of the following.

- Ask God for a ministry partner if you do not have one already.

- Spend time daily and weekly discipling and enjoying your children.

- Brainstorm ways to partner with God's team wherever you work and bless each other's work and pray for each other.

_____

_____

_____

32

PITFALLS

We need to be aware of the pitfalls that can distract or hinder us from planting churches. Sometimes the enemy uses strategies that are clearly sin or evil, but sometimes he will use good things to distract us from God's best for us or for those we want to reach. Many of the following pitfalls can also be great blessings if we exercise wisdom.

1. Social work, NGOs, and businesses

The preaching of the Word and some kind of service have always gone together. Historically, people serving cross-culturally have built schools, hospitals, clinics, and businesses to bless their communities. However, many institutions that started with the priority of sharing the Word have gradually shifted their priorities to elevate the practical service above sharing the gospel. The apostles faced this challenge as well, and their solution was to appoint people whose main job was to care for the practical needs of the people so that they, as church planters and apostles, could concentrate on prayer and the ministry of the Word.

Act 6:1–4: "*Now in these days when the disciples were increasing in number, a complaint by the Hellenists arose against the Hebrews because their widows were being neglected in the daily distribution. And the twelve summoned the full number of the disciples and said, 'It is not right that we should give up preaching the word of God to serve tables. Therefore, brothers, pick out from among you seven men of good repute, full of the Spirit and of wisdom, whom we will appoint to this duty. But we will devote ourselves to prayer and to the ministry of the word.'*"

Paul was a tentmaker. The work he did to earn money was so closely intertwined with his church planting work that the two could not be separated. Paul's model seems to be the best for the times in which we live since many countries that need the gospel will not allow foreigners to live within their borders without having a job. Paul left this important advice to his disciple Timothy shortly before he was executed.

2 Timothy 4:1–2 *"I charge you in the presence of God and of Christ Jesus, who is to judge the living and the dead, and by his appearing and his kingdom: preach the word; be ready in season and out of season; reprove, rebuke, and exhort, with complete patience and teaching."*

2. Discussions

There are some discussions in which missionaries and theologians need to participate because they shape the future of missions. Praise God for the good things that have happened during the last century regarding missions to the unreached. It is important that workers from all over the world continue to communicate in order to hear what the Holy Spirit says.

However, there are also many useless and hurtful discussions that do not glorify God, but rather hinder church planters from concentrating on planting churches. Some of these discussions are related to different approaches to best reach the unreached peoples. These conversations are great as long as the participants are building each other up, but attacking each other and destroying relationships should be avoided.

Sometimes workers gossip about and slander one another instead of confronting the situation or person directly or overlooking the offense. Do not get involved in such talks. Do everything you can to build up relationships with other workers and pray for each other and bless each other.

1 Timothy 1:6 *"Certain persons, by swerving from these, have wandered away into vain discussion."*

1 Corinthians 11:16 *"If anyone is inclined to be contentious, we have no such practice, nor do the churches of God."*

3. Lies from the devil

Sometimes the devil uses lies to hinder the gospel from penetrating a certain people group or a certain city with the good news. The word of God is our weapon to come against such lies as it says that people from all tribes and tongues and languages will worship the Lord.

Revelation 5:9 "*And they sang a new song, saying, 'Worthy are you to take the scroll and to open its seals, for you were slain, and by your blood you ransomed people for God from every tribe and language and people and nation.'*"

For many decades, the devil has tried to make Christians believe that Muslims would never follow Jesus. In the beginning, the devil made people believe that workers could not even enter certain Muslim countries to share the good news. Praise God that Christians did overcome this lie, and people are now sharing the good news in every country of the world. Then the devil tried to make people believe that Muslims would never come to the Lord and that people should not waste time and energy trying to reach them. We know of thousands of Muslims who have found Jesus in different parts of the world. Next, the devil spread lies that hundreds of thousands of Muslims had already come to the Lord so that Christians did not need to go to Muslim countries anymore. When I was preparing to go to North Africa, I was asked why I would still go there because websites were claiming that hundreds of house churches were in place in that city and country. This wasn't true, and it kept people from considering certain countries or cities because they thought those places had already been reached. We still are somewhat affected by this deception, but in many cases people have overcome this kind of thinking.

4. Internet

We all enjoy the blessing of the Internet and the connection it brings to people all over the world. It is also a great tool for sharing Jesus with people in countries that are difficult to access. But this great blessing can also be a curse when we spend more time on the Internet than sharing the gospel. We must be careful not to spend more time on the Internet than with our friends who need the gospel.

5. Other workers or expatriate community

Unity and sharing each other's burden as workers on God's team are great blessings. However, we must balance the times of "filling" with other workers and the times of "pouring out" into our unbelieving friends.

6. Ministries and other good things that are not directly related to your calling

Good things can hinder us in fulfilling the calling that God has put on our life and can become an enemy of His best for us. If you are called to a pioneer church planting ministry, then be careful not to be side-tracked by other ministries.

7. The tension between open fields and hard soil

The Lord lets a church planter live in a holy tension. On one hand, Jesus tells us that the harvest is ripe and that we should bring it in.

John 4:35 *"Do you not say, 'There are yet four months, then comes the harvest'? Look, I tell you, lift up your eyes, and see that the fields are white for harvest."*

On the other hand, we have the clear commandment to share Jesus with all tribes, including those that are very resistant to the gospel.

Matthew 28:19 *"Go therefore and make disciples of all nations, baptizing them in the name of the Father and of the Son and of the Holy Spirit."*

The Lord encourages us to see where the fields are ripe and then to go there and bring the harvest in. In the past, we have missed some of these "ripe fields" because we didn't send enough workers to these places where the harvest was indeed ripe. In 1989 in West Africa, the Arab government initiated an ethnic cleansing of a Muslim unreached people group because of their ethnic background. Thousands of people were killed, and tens of thousands became refugees. While the church gave some help initially, intentional church planting only started about seven years later. The Lord made a harvest ripe but there were no workers to bring it in. We probably missed a great opportunity to see hundreds of people enter the kingdom because no church planters were available to bring the good news to these people when they were most open.

A similar situation exists in Sudan. The Muslim tribes in Darfur and the Nuba Mountains have suffered so much. In the spring of 2013, I got a note from a friend who was visiting one of the camps in which these refugees live. He said, "Many tribes are very open to hear the gospel." Where are the harvesters that will help these people understand what it means to follow Jesus? We are in danger right now of missing an open window from the Lord. "Open your eyes and see the fields are ready for harvesting now."

Praise God that today we are seeing much more fruit than ever before in history among many unreached tribes, even Muslim tribes, all over the world. We live in exciting times as the end of the world draws nearer, and we have the promise in Joel 2 that the Lord will pour out his Spirit. At the same time, people must share the gospel on hard ground with patience and endurance so that at the appointed time, these dry fields will be become ready as well for a great harvest. After many years of the faithful work and prayer of thousands of saints, the Arab world is starting to become fertile. It seems to be one of the hardest soils for the gospel, and it needs workers who will faithfully sow God's word by faith. The Lord looks for patient workers who are willing to lay down their lives for some of the least reached peoples of the world, with great expectation that the Lord would start a mighty work through them.

8. Reporting accurately

It is possible that the unexpressed pressure or expressed expectations from yourself, churches, supporters, and other people to be successful in planting churches can tempt us to report inaccurately and exaggerate the success of our ministry. If the dead have been raised and thousands of people saved, share this for the glory of God. However, if we share information or stories that have not been proven and verified, we are not living in God's truth. During my time in prison when God revealed hidden sin in my heart, He reminded me of times when I had reported fruitfulness in ministry without the verification of other witnesses. Through worship and intimacy with God, the Holy Spirit will help us speak about God's mighty works authentically.

9. Neglecting your physical health

Our body is the temple of the Holy Spirit, and we are asked to take care of it because God Himself lives in it. We should not use it for sexual immorality, excessive eating or drinking, or any other thing that destroys it. We must make time for healthy eating and regular exercise.

1 Corinthians 6:19 "*Or do you not know that your body is a temple of the Holy Spirit within you, whom you have from God?*"

We need to learn how to discipline our bodies and control them and not give room to fleshly passions.

Romans 6:12 "*Let not sin therefore reign in your mortal body, to make you obey its passions.*"

1 Corinthians 9:27 "*But I discipline my body and keep it under control . . .*"

1 Corinthians 6:20 ". . . *So glorify God in your body.*"

1 Corinthians 6:13 "*The body is not meant for sexual immorality, but for the Lord, and the Lord for the body.*"

CHALLENGE

Choose at least one of the following.

- Circle the pitfalls that are a struggle for you:

  1. Wrong priorities of work and ministry
  2. Distracting discussions and debates
  3. Believing lies that hinder a country or people group from access to the gospel
  4. Internet
  5. Other foreign workers
  6. Good things that can distract from God's best thing
  7. Tension between open fields and hard soil
  8. Reporting accurately
  9. Neglecting your physical health

Choose one pitfall and ask God what you should do to grow in this area. Write His answer below:

_____

_____

_____

- Track your time for one week. Take note of the amount of time you spend on work, distracting discussions, the Internet, non-church planting ministries, and visiting with other workers and compare it to the time you spend with locals doing church planting activities.

- Find a partner and commit to exercising with him once per week.

- Have you learned how to eat a healthy, balanced diet in your new culture? If not, find someone who has and get ideas from him or her. Plan one to two weeks of meals with your new ideas.

- When was the last time you set aside time to pray and asked God if you are still doing what He wants you to do? Confess any fears you might have first so that your heart is totally willing to act on whatever He might say.

33

YOUR RACE WITH GOD

In whatever position and life situation the Lord has put us, as followers of Christ we are called to influence the world in which we live with God's love and the beautiful message of Jesus Christ.

I believe that there are four categories of people who might read this book. I would like to write a few thoughts to all four of them.

1. People who have not yet started the race

We are never too young or too old to start racing with our Lord. As long as we live on this earth, the Lord has a special plan for each of us. He often uses small children and older people until their last breath to demonstrate His glory.

God started to use Moses when he was eighty years old; Caleb proclaimed at the age of eighty or more that he still felt strong and mighty to take the land through the power that lived in him. Abraham had his first son when he was nearly one hundred years old, and Sarah gave birth to her son in her very advanced age. A person is never too old to be a part of what God is doing and to walk in His steps, and at the same time, one is never too young to participate with God in His work.

Psalm 8:2 "Out of the mouth of babes and infants, you have established strength because of your foes, to still the enemy and the avenger."

Jeremiah 1:6–7 "*Then I said, 'Ah, Lord GOD! Behold, I do not know how to speak, for I am only a youth.' But the LORD said to me, 'Do not say, "I am only a youth;" for to all to whom I send you, you shall go, and whatever I command you, you shall speak.'"*

2. People who face challenges in their walk with God

Are you asking yourself, "How did I get myself into this?" Is it hard to remember why you started doing what you are doing? Do you need God to issue "the call" again? You are not alone! Anyone who gives his entire life for the advancement of the kingdom of God finds himself in seasons during which these questions and others pop up quite a bit more than every once in a while. God is not surprised by or frustrated with these questions. We know this because He wrote the answers in His book long before we were born. He is spurring us on and encouraging us to finish well. The Lord gives us the amazing promise that it is He who will do it through us.

Philippians 2:13 *"For it is God who works in you, both to will and to work for his good pleasure."*

Philippians 1:6 *"And I am sure of this, that he who began a good work in you will bring it to completion at the day of Jesus Christ."*

God Himself gave you the desire to serve Him, and He will also give you the will to bring it to completion. Do not let present struggles or challenges or failures lead you towards total frustration! Always remember the Lord is strong when you are weak. He might allow us to come into situations where we feel weak so that we remember Him and put our trust in Him. Every challenging situation is a chance to grow and to become more and more like Jesus.

Commit your life and your whole situation to the Lord, and He will be your strength. You will come out of every challenge strengthened by the grace of Jesus and for His honor and glory.

3. People who are thriving

What a joy it is to serve the Lord and to walk daily in His presence. This doesn't mean that such people don't face times when they feel tired or discouraged, but there is a general happiness in their daily walk with Jesus. The Lord transforms them continuously more and more into His image, and their ministry is blessed by the Lord and shows visible fruit. This is the desire of our Lord, and this is how we glorify God.

John 15:8, Jesus says, *"By this my Father is glorified, that you bear much fruit and so prove to be my disciples."*

During seasons of success, happiness, or flourishing, we must guard against a haughty heart or becoming proud. Proverbs 16:18 warns us that "*pride precedes destruction; an arrogant spirit appears before a fall.*" (ISV) The way to be great in the kingdom of God is to become the least. " *. . . If anyone would be first, he must be last of all and servant of all.*" (Mark 9:35)

So as you are thriving with Jesus, I encourage you to ask God to show you a few people in whom you might invest so that they could grow in their faith as well. These might be new believers that you disciple and help to bear fruit, or it might be leaders that you mentor to help move ahead in leadership.

4. People who are discouraged or who have even left the race

There are different reasons people walk away from God, and the parable of the four types of soil gives us some insight into these reasons. Some leave the faith when struggles and difficulties come. Others are drawn away by the pleasures of the world. Still others probably never really count the cost of laying down their lives and living for Jesus. In life, very difficult things happen that we will not be able to understand, but God has given us assurance in these very circumstances:

Romans 8:28 "*And we know that for those who love God all things work together for good, for those who are called according to his purpose.*"

This is what God promised us in His Word, and it is fully true even when we don't have answers for everything that happens on earth. One day, when we enjoy eternal life with Jesus, the Father, millions of angels, and believers from every nation, tongue, and tribe, we will fully understand. For now our understanding is in part as it is written:

1 Corinthians 13:12 "*For now we see in a mirror dimly, but then face to face. Now I know in part; then I shall know fully, even as I have been fully known.*"

So, if you are discouraged or have left the race, come back to Jesus and surrender your whole life to Him. Never let any situation take you away from the wondrous love of Jesus. He waits for you and is eager to take you back. As long as you breathe, there is still time to come back to Jesus and continue your race with Him.

CONCLUSION

The Bible tells us that all followers of Jesus are chosen by the King of kings, who created the heavens and earth, to finish the race with Jesus and make this the ultimate goal of their lives. If you are looking for adventure and meaning in your life, sign up for the race with God.

1 Peter 2:9 *"But you are a chosen race, a royal priesthood, a holy nation, a people for his own possession, that you may proclaim the excellencies of him who called you out of darkness into his marvelous light."*

2 Corinthians 5:20 *"Therefore, we are ambassadors for Christ, God making his appeal through us. We implore you on behalf of Christ, be reconciled to God."*

You belong to God, and you are His. God Himself calls you a royal priest and His ambassador. He considers us worthy to represent Him wherever He has planted us. He has made us heirs of His kingdom, co-heirs with Christ, and therefore we have access to all His riches in the heavenly places. We are vessels through which God wants to bestow blessing and power on all the peoples of the earth.

In 1 Corinthians 9:26, Paul says that he is running his race, and he makes it clear that he is not running aimlessly. In Philippians 3:14, he said that he hasn't finished his race yet, but presses on towards the goal that is before him.

Paul longs to finish well so that he can run across the finish line and be with His Lord and Savior Jesus Christ. And he is willing to do anything during his race on earth to invite as many as possible into the salvation of Jesus.

> Our best and deepest experiences with God often come when we face situations so difficult that we ourselves do not see a way out.

Philippians 1:21–24 *"For to me to live is Christ, and to die is gain. If I am to live in the flesh, that means fruitful labor for me. Yet which I shall choose I cannot tell. I am hard pressed between the two. My desire is to depart and be with Christ, for that is far better. But to remain in the flesh is more necessary on your account."*

Our best and deepest experiences with God often come when we face situations so difficult that we ourselves do not see a way out. In this place, the closeness and intimacy with God is indescribable. Giving God our lives will never ever disappoint us. The quality of the satisfying love, joy, and peace that He offers us in the valleys of despair far outweighs the answers that we sometimes seek more passionately than God Himself.

2 Corinthians 4:17 *"For this light momentary affliction is preparing for us an eternal weight of glory beyond all comparison."*

I experienced this to be true when I was in prison, and I would not hesitate for one second to wholeheartedly recommend running the race with God. I testify with all my heart that it is the most exciting thing one can do with his life. I would never exchange sweet fellowship with Jesus for anything else.

APPENDIX 1

FAMILY DEVOTIONAL

Some people like to worship the Lord alone, and others prefer doing it as a community. Both ways are important and need to be practiced. "A family that prays together, stays together," I once saw written on a picture. As a family, we have gone through different ways and seasons of worshiping the Lord together. When I was in prison, the Lord showed me a new way to worship Him together as a family before facing the joys and challenges of our daily routine.

Every morning before we have breakfast as a family, we go through this devotional. The whole family recites the text in Ecclesiastes and one person then reads the rest. After this, we pray together as a family and start the day with our Lord Jesus. This happens after each of us has had his personal time with the Lord in the morning. In the evening, we read a Bible text together and discuss questions or issues from our morning and evening Scripture readings.

The following is an example of a way to lift up the Lord daily as a family. The main references are Ecclesiastes 9:7–10 and Exodus 20:12.

Ecclesiastes 9:7–10[5]

"Go, eat your food with gladness,
and drink your wine with a joyful heart
for God has already approved what you do.
Always be clothed in white,
and always anoint your head with oil.
Enjoy life with your wife, whom you love,
all the days of this meaningless life
that God has given you under the sun—
all your meaningless days.
For this is your lot in life
and in your toilsome labor under the sun.
Whatever your hand finds to do,
do it with all your might,
for in the realm of the dead, where you are going,
there is neither working nor planning
nor knowledge nor wisdom."

Exodus 20:12

"Honor your father and your mother, so that you may live long in the land the Lord your God is giving you."

1. Go, eat your food with gladness, and drink your wine with a joyful heart

Romans 14:17–18 *"For the kingdom of God is not a matter of eating and drinking, but of righteousness, peace and joy in the Holy Spirit, because anyone who serves Christ in this way is pleasing to God and receives human approval."*

We should be joyful people and families as the Lord gives us our daily food and meets our daily needs. At the same time, the kingdom of God is not just about physical things, but about righteousness, peace, and joy in the Holy Spirit. As followers of Jesus, we need to train ourselves by remembering daily that the righteousness, peace, and joy of the Lord never changes.

---

5 Scripture quotations in this chapter are taken from The Holy Bible, New International Version, NIV Copyright © 1973, 1978, 1984, 2011 by Biblica, Inc.

2. For God has already approved what you do

Psalm 37:4 "*Take delight in the Lord, and he will give you the desires of your heart.*"

Psalm 20:4 "*May he give you the desire of your heart and make all your plans succeed.*"

Proverbs 16:3 "*Commit to the Lord whatever you do, and he will establish your plans.*"

What an amazing promise from the Lord to us as we seek to build his kingdom! Favor means that the Lord looks at us with pleasure and joy when we worship and obey Him. God is pleased by whatever we do from the place of our worship of Him.

3. Always be clothed in white

Isaiah 61:10 "*For he has clothed me with garments of salvation and arrayed me in a robe of his righteousness . . .*"

Romans 13:14 ". . . *clothe yourselves with the Lord Jesus Christ, and do not think about how to gratify the desires of the flesh.*"

Always be washed by the blood of Jesus and be clothed in His righteousness. Always means every day. We must make sure that our hearts are washed daily. The devil wants to destroy our purity. When we are not walking in purity, we put our families, marriages, teams, and other relationships in danger and leave them vulnerable to attack from the enemy.

4. Always anoint your head with oil

Ephesians 5:18 ". . . *be filled with the Spirit.*"

Psalm 23:5 ". . . *You anoint my head with oil; my cup overflows.*"

Always be filled with the Holy Spirit. This is a great encouragement to be filled with the Holy Spirit at all times. We need to seek this filling of the Holy Spirit daily. We need His guidance when we share the gospel with those around us. We need His presence to sustain us. We need His grace so that we can thrive in our daily work. He wants to reveal to us the secrets of His will for our current situation, and He wants to do His works through us every day.

5. Enjoy life with your wife, whom you love, all the days of this meaningless life

Ephesians 5:25–26 "*Husbands, love your wives, just as Christ loved the church and gave himself up for her to make her holy . . .*"

Be an example to others of a happy marriage and family. Let people feel and see the joy in your house when they enter. Let them see that you are in love with your wife.

6. Honor your father and your mother, so that you may live long in the land the Lord your God is giving you

Ephesians 6:1 "*Children, obey your parents in the Lord, for this is right.*"

Ideally, children honor their father and mother in response to the experience of their love and the understanding that they are seeking God's best for their lives. The way we treat children and raise them to obey us as parents is a very powerful testimony. A godly family speaks very strongly to the world. Invite other families into your life, so they can see how the members of a redeemed family treat one another.

7. Whatever your hand finds to do, do it with all your might

Colossians 3:23 "*Whatever you do, work at it with all your heart, as working for the Lord, not for human masters.*"

Romans 12:11 "*Never be lacking in zeal, but keep your spiritual fervor, serving the Lord.*"

This reminds our family daily that we want to be fully committed to what the Lord has called us to do. The details of the call might vary in different stages of our lives, but the commitment and the eagerness and the zeal with which we do it doesn't change. Do everything you do with all your might, strength, and heart.

APPENDIX 2

FIFTEEN PRINCIPLES OF DISCIPLE MAKING MOVEMENTS (DMMS)[6]

The aim of each pioneering work is for large percentages of or even the entire people group to turn to Jesus and be transformed by obeying His words through the power of the Holy Spirit. Though many different approaches and strategies to start movements for Jesus exist, it seems that there are components that are common to many of the movements so far. Listed below are components that I think are the most important.

Work of the Holy Spirit	While human principles can facilitate and prepare for a movement, it is always the work of the Holy Spirit that accomplishes it.
Sincere Prayer	Sincere prayer is the foundation of a movement. Church planters and their partners spend a lot of time in prayer asking God to reveal His power.

---

6   Disciple Making Movements (DMMs) are also known as Church Planting Movements (CPMs) or Jesus Movements (JMs).

Massive Sowing	Broad sowing of God's word must take place. This includes personal witnessing and a wide range of media like books, TV, Internet, film, video, radio, and so on.
Transformed Lives	Believers express their love for Jesus by inviting Him into all aspects of their daily lives and by worshipping Him in culturally appropriate forms. They experience a growing love for God's word and an ongoing transformation into the image of Jesus by the Holy Spirit.
Obedience	Discipleship has a strong focus on obedience. New believers immediately learn how to be nourished by hearing or reading the word of God and applying what they have understood in their daily lives.
Group-orientation	Believers learn how to live out kingdom truths within their social networks. The members of the group help each other apply what they are learning. They express the love of Jesus to each other by practicing the "one another commandments" and bearing each other's burdens.
Person of Peace	People of peace open new social networks for the gospel. These men and women invite their extended family or social network into the kingdom so that groups of believers are formed almost immediately.
Ecclesia	Believers gather according to pre-existing social networks such as families. They meet on a very regular basis for prayer, Bible study, worship and fellowship and are led by an eldership.

Indigenous Lay Leadership	The leaders of these groups are all indigenous and lay workers. They model to others how to lead groups while working in their professions and therefore open the doors for unlimited multiplication as others can easily follow their examples.
Multiplication	Multiplication is part of the DNA right from the beginning. Each person who attends a group is asked to share what they have learned with another person by the time the group meets again.
Mutual Accountability	Accountability happens within the community. Believers hold each other accountable to obey what they learned in the last group meeting and to share it with at least one non-believer.
Intentional Mentoring from Outside	Mentoring of the key leaders is done by experienced church planters who are not part of the people group that is being reached for Christ. The mentors cast vision and help the key leaders to accomplish the vision for their people group to be reached with the gospel.
Vision for Expansion	A clear vision for the way the movement can grow and reach the rest of their people group needs to be present. Eventually, the leaders cast an expanded vision to reach neighboring unreached tribes as well, and the believers take ownership of this vision.
On-the-job Training	Emerging leaders are trained on-the-job. They are not extracted from their communities by long-term Bible school based training.

Persecution and Suffering

Harsh persecution and intense suffering are part of most DMMs. However, the disciples do not view this persecution as the end, but rather as a divine springboard for more boldness and growth. Instead of avoiding it, they embrace it.

APPENDIX 3

GLOSSARY

African Muslims African Muslims are Muslim by religion, but come from many different African tribes and often do not speak Arabic.

animists The belief in the existence of individual spirits that inhabit natural objects and phenomena.

Arab Muslims Muslims who are from an Arab tribe and also speak Arabic.

bush taxi A special taxi used in Africa to travel to remote areas.

contextualization To share the message of Jesus in a culturally adapted way (to contextualize the message) so that it makes sense to the people that hear it.

cross-cultural worker A person who leaves their home culture and moves into another culture to share Jesus. This often but not always involves learning a new culture and a new language.

educational centers Centers where people can learn different things like languages, computer skills, and other educational subjects. Cross-cultural workers can bless their host culture by starting such centers.

English centers Centers where people learn English—often adults.

ethnic cleansing The systematic elimination of an ethnic group or groups from a region or society, as by deportation, forced emigration, or genocide.

folk Islam It describes forms of Islam that incorporate native folk beliefs and practices that are often occult.

furlough A time that overseas workers spend in their home country to renew contacts and prayer support for their ministry.

genocide Deliberate killing of people who belong to a particular racial, political, or cultural group.

house churches Groups of people who meet either in their houses or in any other places where they feel safe to worship Jesus. They meet in usual places where normal socialization happens and not in "church buildings."

Islam Second largest religion in the world next to Christianity.

Jesus film A film that shows the life of Jesus starting from the account recorded in the Gospel of Luke (can be watched on jesusfilmmedia.org).

Koran	The holy book of Muslims.
local people	The citizens of the country. A worker in a different country often refers to local people as those that he is reaching with the gospel.
Mary Magdalene movie	The life of Jesus as seen through the eyes of Mary Magdalene. The film is especially useful when reaching out to women (can be watched on jesusfilmmedia.org).
MBB	Muslim Background Believer.
missionary	A follower of Jesus who speaks to other people about his Savior. The term is often used to describe cross-cultural workers. The term is traditionally used to describe someone whose only identity in a culture is planting churches. Usually, this person lives in a culture other than his home culture.
Muslim	A person who is part of the religion of Islam.
NGO	Non-governmental organization.
planting churches	Doing evangelism and discipleship for the purpose of people coming into the kingdom of God, worshipping together and obeying the teachings of Jesus. These new fellowships should also reproduce themselves by sharing this good news with others. It has nothing to do with a building.
people group	Ethno-linguistic groupings of people. A group of people with a unique ethnicity or language that distinguishes it from others.

people movement	When a significant part of a people group turns to Jesus. This is the ultimate goal and hope for most church planters.
run-bag	A small bag that always stays packed and ready to go if you only have a few minutes before you must leave.
sending base	A sending base is an office in the worker's home country that facilitates his going to a different country.
sending/home church	A body of believers that sends workers to other places with the goal of spreading the gospel. They pray for the workers and are pastorally responsible for them and may support them financially.
sending organization	An organization that is often international and facilitates the sending of workers to different countries or areas.
unreached people group	A distinguished people group that has no or little access to the gospel of Jesus Christ.
worker	In this book, this term is a shortened version of "cross-cultural worker."
YWAM	Youth with a Mission is a large mission organization, which, among other things, offers training in discipleship and evangelism all over the world.